Property of Diane Eusepi

P9-CSE-653

Flying Geese & Partridge Feet

Flying Geese & Partridge Feet

*More Mittens from
Up North & Down East*

By Robin Hansen
With Janetta Dexter

Down East Books

In memory of Albert Miller,
who was dedicated to preserving
the good mitten patterns of our grandparents

Copyright © 1986 by Robin Hansen
ISBN 0-89272-214-2
Library of Congress Catalog Card No. 85-72923
Cover design by Bonnie Bishop
Composition by Typeworks, Inc., Belfast, Maine
Printed by Capital City Press, Montpelier, Vt.

9 8 7 6 5 4

Down East Books / Camden, Maine

Contents

(Color photographs of mittens and caps, pages 65 through 68)

Introduction

Fox & Geese & Fences was a collection of mittens and mitten traditions from old Yankee families of Maine, mostly of British extraction. This book expands on that collection and includes some of the other folk mitten traditions in Maine and Canada's Atlantic Provinces.

Fox & Geese & Fences contained all Robin knew about Maine mittens at the time. Since its publication in 1983, women from all over New England and eastern Canada have contributed more and more information about how people from the gentle western coasts of Europe and Britain adapted their knitting to the often bitter cold of eastern North America—and how they kept their hands and feet warm.

Lumberjacks in Maine—men alone in the woods—knit their own plain gray wool mittens and heelless tube socks. Women in both interior Maine and New Brunswick knit Double-rolled Mittens that carried thick strands of fleece along behind the knit. Logger John Richardson, of Mariaville, Maine, covered plain white mittens with a thick sewn-on wool pile, then dyed them black to hide the dirt and make them show up on snow.

Other women hooked half-inch-long yarn "fur" into cloth mittens. In hard times, old coating was laid out and a mother or grandmother traced around hands and made sewn mittens—"a perfect fit, and so warm" remembers a woman who grew up in Maine.

Many of the mittens here have other than English roots. Acadian women work fleurs-de-lis into their mittens and knit the whole mitten differently from their Anglo neighbors. The hardy women of Newfoundland and Labrador knit waves and caribou designs into theirs, as well as a diamond pattern that has roots reaching straight across northern Europe to Estonia. The Moravian missionaries in Labrador taught Inuit women traditional Norwegian patterns; Inuit knitters still knit them, using the quick-fingered European technique of knitting, while most of the rest of the area uses the English technique.

In Nova Scotia and New Brunswick, women "double knit" two-colored mittens covered with small geometric designs, like (and unlike) those known in Maine.

Here is the second collection of warm traditional mittens, passed to you in the new tradition—by book—often in the words of the kind knitters who showed us how. They have been unearthed not by us but by people who make them or remember them and want the techniques remembered too and passed down. We have been a clearing house to receive and pass on information that other knitters have developed over generations.

Please try all that appeal to you, whether because they're from your province or state or because they intrigue you for one reason or another. But when you've sampled to your heart's content, we do hope you will choose one or two to make on your own, ones that you'll come to know inside out, to which you'll add your own little fillips and improvements. And we hope you will knit these one or two patterns for everyone in your family for a hundred years and teach them to your granddaughters.

In this way, you will become part of the folk process, and the good, warm patterns of our grandmothers will be carried on in new generations.

When you have done this, you can throw away

this book and instead keep a little bag of your
''pattens'' in your knitting basket. Then you too
will be a traditional knitter.

Good knitting and warm hands to you!

—Robin Hansen
—Janetta Dexter

General Instructions and Sources of Materials

The most general instructions we can give you are to ask you to *read the instructions* and *follow them*. These are old patterns that have been around for generations, and all the different ways of doing things here have a reason behind them. If you don't do it right, you'll probably do it wrong, waste your own time and materials, and wonder what happened. So do read and study the diagrams carefully.

These patterns include many odd ways of doing things, which are usually only learned by sitting next to someone and watching. To simulate that immediacy, we've made picture series for some of the harder-to-explain ideas. Others, including some tricky increases, are graphed. Don't let the graphs frighten you; they're just another way of getting across an idea, another way of drawing. Look at them closely and read the instructions that accompany them, and you'll see that they're usually easier to understand than the text.

Materials

Most of the mittens, caps, and socks here are made with worsted weight yarns (medium weight in U.K. and Canada).

Because we're doing a lot of border-hopping in this book, we've used both Canadian and American yarns. We've also tried to use wool from mills in Atlantic Canada and New England, as these yarns were most often used in traditional knitting. Even today, many families with sheep take their fleeces to a local mill to be exchanged for spun yarn, and the mills rely upon these family shipments to supply them. We used mostly yarn from Briggs & Little Woolen Mills, Ltd., Harvey Station, New Brunswick, E0H 1H0, Canada, and Bartlettyarns, Harmony, ME 04942, supplementing with commercial wool yarn from Brunswick Yarns (U.S.)

and Paton's (Canada) when it seemed right.

Although we've called for worsted weight yarn, we realize that even in the United States, where this term makes sense, there is a great deal of variation in yarns. Briggs & Little has two yarns that fall into that size range: 2/12 and 2/8, which proprietor John Little says were once called sock (2/8) and mitten (2/12) yarn, with the lighter yarn used for mittens. We've used 2/8 for some of the mittens, including Shepherd's Plaid Gloves. The 2/8 makes a fiercely durable handcovering, a little too rough for ladies and too stiff for small children. The 2/12 can be knit as tightly as 8 stitches per inch without strain and as loosely as 6 stitches per inch for caps. It fills the bill nicely for women and children as well as for dressier mittens and gloves.

Bartlettyarns has comparable wool yarns. Their 2-ply Homespun knits like Briggs & Little's 2/8. It comes in solid dyed colors and natural sheep's colors. Their 2-ply Fisherman Yarn, which comes in heather mixtures and natural sheep colors and mixes, knits up a dight heavier than Briggs & Little's 2/12.

Christopher Farms (Richmond, ME 04357) has a sportweight yarn a bit lighter, almost a fingering yarn, which is even lighter than B & L's 2/12. Charity Hill Farm's 2-ply worsted (available through W.E.B.S., P.O. Box 349, Amherst, MA 01002) is a marvelous light worsted yarn to work with. I knitted the green example of Mrs. Martin's Finger Mitts with this yarn and found it the closest American equivalent to B & L's 2/12 I've yet seen. One can get a color card from any of these mills and distributors by writing for it.

If you would like to knit a true Newfoundland mitten with homespun yarn but don't spin, there are many handspinners around. Check with fiber-arts stores or yarn stores, or ask at sheep shows and county fairs.

If these lovely, natural, and rough yarns are not available and you don't want to wait for an order to come by mail, you can still knit folk mittens from New England and Maritime Canada. Commercial wool yarns like Brunswick Yarns Germantown Knitting Worsted, or Coats and Clarks Red Heart Wool Knitting Worsted work just fine, give a softer finished product, and often have a wider selection of colors. They are comparable in weight to B & L's 2/12 or the Charity Hill worsted and can be knit as tightly as 8 to 8.5 stitches per inch with good effect. As for authenticity, bear in mind that many traditional knitters have thrown out the idea of using wool altogether and knit only in synthetics, so you'll be one step more traditional than that.

The baby mittens in the Chicky Feet section and the Flying Geese gloves are knit of what Americans call "sportweight" yarn and what is called "finger-ing" throughout Canada. ("Fingering" in the U.S. is always even finer—also called "baby yarn.") They too are knitted of wool, generally Brunswick Yarns Pomfret or Lady Galt Kroy by Paton and Baldwin. The gray in the Tiny Diamond mittens is a sportweight (Canadian: fingering) from Bartlett-yarns; it looks skinnier than the commercial sport yarns when strands are compared, but in fact it has less loft and knits up a tad thicker. Mix it in with care, or use two of its natural colors in combination.

Fleece, pencil rovings, and one-inch rovings can be ordered from Briggs & Little Woolen Mill, Ltd., Harvey Station, York County, E0H 1H0, NB, Canada, or from Bartlettyarns, Harmony, ME 04942.

On the subject of wool versus synthetics, I repeat a story told before, in *Fox and Geese and Fences*: In the first snowfall one winter, our children burst out of the house in whatever winter clothes they could find—last year's jackets, unmatched boot socks and mittens, and caps that were too big or too small.

About ten minutes later, my seven-year-old was back inside, in tears. "My hand is so cold!" he wept, shaking it splashily.

On that hand he was wearing a mitten made of a synthetic yarn. It was soaked like a wet mop, it was heavy, and it was freezing cold.

The other hand, which emerged from its mitten rosy and steamy warm (I'm not exaggerating), was wearing a wool double-knit mitten, like the ones you'll find in this book. It was covered with caked-on wet snow. But it was warm and dry inside.

Some knitters tell me wool is harsh to knit with. If you think so, choose a softer wool. Not all wool is scratchy. Commercial worsteds like Brunswick Germantown are not. Other women who love synthetics tell me you can throw the synthetic mittens in the washer, launder them, then throw them in the dryer. I haven't yet figured out why this should be an important feature for anything but a baby mitten. Winter is usually over before mittens get washed in our house. If it's an issue with you, there are many preshrunk Superwash wools on the market that can stand this kind of treatment without shrinking.

Of course, wool does shrink. Some knitters overcome this problem by washing the yarn in the skein in hot soapy water and rinsing it in cold *before* knitting it, thus preshrinking it. Others knit the mitten slightly longer than the hand, to be shrunk informally in use and on the radiator.

Shrinking is part of the wool's natural defense

against cold and wet, and actually improves a garment's weather resistance. Fishermen's mittens, a tight, single-knit mitten once worn all along the north Atlantic coast, are meant to be felted and shrunk in use. They are knit inches too long and very wide.

Equipment

Needle sizes are given in American standard (U.S.) and Canadian (Can.) sizes. In case you live in Oslo or the Himalayas, here are approximate equivalents for metric needle sizes:

AMERICAN	CANADIAN	METRIC
0	14	2
1	13	2.5
2	11	3
3	10	3
4	9	3.5
5	8	4
6	7	4.5

Knitting needle conversions are always approximate, but the important thing is to have the right number of stitches per inch. Most yarn stores—even yarn departments in big discount stores—will usually let you knit a two-inch square to check your tension if you bring your own yarn. If they don't, shop elsewhere.

Gauge

Please don't ever knit anything without making a test gauge to check your tension (the tightness of your knitting). Most people knit at about the same tension on a given size knitting needle with a given size yarn but maybe the pattern designer doesn't. Maybe in a double-knit, you won't.

Do this by casting on about 15 stitches on the same size needle and with the same yarn you plan to use for your project. Knit back and forth with stockinette stitch in the pattern you plan to use.

If your flat knitting differs from your knitting-in-the-round, cast on 21 stitches on three double-pointed needles—seven to a needle—and knit around in the pattern you'll use.

Knit about two inches. Then, push and pull the piece a little, flatten it out, and measure it across the stitches in the middle where there's no pull from either edge, the needles, or casting on. Count how many stitches are within one inch. Count half-stitches too. If you're in doubt, count across two inches and divide by two.

If there is a half-stitch too many within your inch, try the next size larger needles. For a half-stitch too few, go to the next size smaller. If you're shy a whole stitch, go down two sizes, and so forth.

Sizes

The sizes are pretty clearly stated in the instructions. What isn't stated is that large children wear small adult-size mittens and caps. And small men's hands fit quite comfortably in women's medium-size mittens.

Men's large is enormous. If I had followed the large size on several locally available patterns, it would have been even more enormous, but I couldn't find anyone with a hand big enough to fit it, so I concluded that their sizing might be off.

To give you some firm numbers to go on, I hereby reveal the measurements on which I've based all my sizing. I got these measurements not from a book, but by trying mittens and gloves on many real people. Length measurement is for the *hand only*, without cuff. All measurements are in inches.

	MITTEN LENGTH	MITTEN WIDTH
BIRTH TO 6 MONTHS	3⅛	2
6 MONTH TO 1 YEAR	3⅜	2¼
2 YEARS	3½	2⅝
3 YEARS	4	2⅘
4 YEARS	4½ to 5	3¼
2 TO 3 YEARS (worsted)	4½ to 5	3¼
4 TO 6 YEARS	5½ to 6	3¼
8 TO 10 YEARS (child's medium)	6½	3½
WOMAN'S SMALL	7	3¾
WOMAN'S MEDIUM	7½	4
MAN'S MEDIUM (adult's medium)	7½	4½
MAN'S LARGE (adult's large)	8	5

Abbreviations

I've kept these to the bare minimum to make the instructions more readable.

Any that aren't included below are explained in the text of the instructions where they are used.

cc	contrast color
dec	decrease
dk	dark
dp	double-pointed, as in dp knitting needles
inc	increase
k	knit
lt	light
mc	main color
no.	number, as in no. 3 knitting needles
p	purl
st, sts	stitch, stitches
Can.	Canadian, as in Can. no. 10 knitting needles
U.S.	American, as in U.S. no. 3 knitting needles

On the graphs, **X** and **O** represent stitches in the contrasting colors, the little squares are stitches in the background color, and a heavy line shows the edge of the mitten, also showing increases and decreases. Largish **X**s that cross squares are decreases.

Note that the large graphs show big holes where the thumb is supposed to go and have the thumb graphed separately. These holes are just an illusion. Mentally insert the first round of the thumb gore in the first round of the hole, and you're all set.

—R.H.

Part One

Practical Woolies from the Interior

Practical Woolies from the Interior

Wool mittens are warm, but a knitted fabric is a mesh, full of holes. The icy wind blows, and being a lazy wind, it will go right through, rather than around, the ordinary wool mitten. All the mitten patterns in this book are old-time inventions to deal with this very aspect of the knitted wool mitten.

One of the most widespread methods is to knit alternating two strands of yarn, so that every hole in the knit is backed with the other strand of yarn. In Dalarna, Sweden, this is done in one color, but in most places, it's done with two, and the colors are alternated to make patterns taken from patchwork and weaving, and given names from the surrounding world. You will find these double-knit patterns in the second part of this book.

But there are other ways of getting rid of or covering the holes. The most usual one in today's world is to cover the mitten with a yellow horsehide mitten or other windproof cover. This solution is like wearing a paper bag over the head to hide problem skin: it solves the problem, but it isn't good looking. It covers up the beautiful mitten.

A mitten can be felted by washing it in hot, soapy water and rinsing it in cold water, vigorously and repeatedly. Fishermen's mittens are treated this way, and shrink into dense, matted handcoverings that are worn wet: the wetness adds to the windproofing and denseness.* The knitting still shows.

In both Europe and America, knitted mittens have been covered with pile, or lined with pile, or lined with tufts or rolls of fleece or loops of wool. These too are handsome solutions. And these are the mittens we offer here, as well as a mitten crocheted on a homemade hook—a method that eliminates all the lacy holes one associates with crochet.

---

*Instructions for Fishermen's Wet Mittens can be found in *Fox & Geese & Fences* (see bibliography).

Double-rolled Mittens

I had spread my mittens under a tree at Norlands Living History Center Heritage Days Festival, to excite interest and conversation and to show off the marvelous warmth and good looks of old-time Maine mittens.

But the reception at Norlands—near Livermore, Maine—was different from the reception at other places, where people exclaim at the mittens' thickness or remember the patterns from their childhood. In the Norlands area, people still knit the traditional mittens, and the response is always, ''Oh, I know someone who knits mittens like that.''

At Norlands I met Beulah Moore, who found my collection of mittens incomplete. ''Don't you have any Double-rolled Mittens?'' she asked, after looking them over. Double-rolled mittens? I'd never heard of them.

Double-rolled Mittens are knit in one color, with a narrow roll of unspun fleece carried behind the work, caught up between stitches. Mrs. Moore showed me how to carry the fleece so that the knitting progresses rapidly, flipping the little bit of fleece over and under the knitting strand with each stitch.

She was unwilling to make me a pair right then, but she did teach me the technique. I was able to play with what she had shown me, so when I saw my first real pair of Double-rolled Mittens in the Maine State Museum, I knew immediately what they were. With Curator Paul Rivard's permission, Mrs. Hattie Stover Brown's mittens are shown here in the black-and-white photo. They were knit is a somewhat finer yarn than I have used, at a tension of seven stitches per inch.

I had just decided that this technique was truly extinct when I met Edna Mower, of Merrimack,

MAINE STATE MUSEUM. PHOTO BY GREGORY HART.

Double-rolled mittens knitted by Hattie Stover Brown in 1897.

New Hampshire, who told me she still knits Double-rolled Mittens and socks. ''I can't imagine why it should be extinct,'' she told me. ''It's really a simple procedure.''

Mrs. Mower grew upon on a farm in Sevogle, New Brunswick, 17 miles upriver from New Castle, in a large family that combined French and Irish, Scottish and English traditions. Her father was the ranger for the region; her mother was a schoolteacher.

''We learned to do everything,'' Mrs. Mower remembers. ''You learned to milk cows and churn butter and knit and crochet and hoe the garden and clean the barns and everything else.'' She grew up making several well-known double-knit patterns that her family taught her, but she learned to make Double-rolled Mittens from a neighbor.

"I remember learning it very well. I probably was about 12. I watched an elderly woman in the neighborhood making them. I watched her and she said, 'Wouldn't you like to learn to do these, too?' I said yes. She said, 'Well, it's a very simple procedure. I card the rolls myself with a pair of cards, then I pull it out very, very thin, you know, and long.' And she said, 'Fine, I'll give you a handful, a great handful of the wool you put on the inside, and you try it yourself and see how you do.' I knit them for my father first, and he showed them around, and everyone seemed to want them.

"I saw this woman taking these pieces of wool and pulling them out and knitting and stopping every little while to make a dozen or so [rolls]. And I thought, 'It's silly to stop and pull these apart when you can do the same thing with pencil roving.' "

Pencil roving comes in big, flat half-pound reels from Briggs & Little in New Brunswick, or from Bartlettyarns in Maine. It's a narrow strip of carded but unspun wool, very thin and light. Some people spin it; others knit it. Some of the women who work at Briggs & Little knit bunches of short bits of it into Newfoundland style Fleece-stuffed Mittens.* Mrs. Mower uses it for Double-rolled Mittens.

Both living women who have shown me this technique have used the over-and-under method that produces something of a thick lattice appearance on the lining and reverses the twist of fleece with each stitch. This is visible on the outside too, if you look closely.

On Mrs. Brown's mittens, however, the twists are all in the same direction, and the lining looks as if each loop between stitches were *wrapped* with a twist of fleece. The twists of fleece lay close, side by side, each fitting neatly against the next and those above and below. To get this effect, one must knit in the Anglo-American right-handed way, throwing the yarn with the right forefinger, flipping the fleece over and over. For this, one can't use a continuous strand, as it would reverse-twist hopelessly around the yarn. One must use a short bit, as Mrs. Brown must have, as Mrs. Moore said one must, and as Mrs. Mower's neighbor did.

My private theory is that the one-way twist with short bits of fleece is the ancestor of the other, and that when clever knitting methods—two-handed stranding and Continental left-handed knitting—came in, not many people figured out how to adapt the old technique to their new method, and it passed almost out of existence. A pity, for the mittens are soft and thick and strong.

When Mrs. Moore first told me about Double-rolled Mittens, she said to use no. 1 or no. 0 needles, but I (1) disbelieved, and (2) decided there were better things to do with my time than knit mittens on no. 0 needles. I assumed that anything knit on such tiny needles must have a tension of about 11 (or more) stitches to the inch, which in this case turned out to be a wrong assumption.

The twist of fleece forces the stitches apart slightly, so that one must use tiny needles even to get a fairly loose tension like six stitches to the inch.

There's no way to keep the fleece from showing through here and there, and in fact, this is part of the mitten's charm. The slightly raggy look is folksy, like gray ragg socks, and tells the world you know a better way of keeping warm.

The shag cuff is a touch hard to pass up. Although easy to apply, it looks smashing, as well as old-

*Instructions for Fleece-stuffed Mittens can be found in *Fox & Geese & Fences* (see bibliography).

fashioned in a very nice way, like the fur blankets in the film *Dr. Zhivago*.

Although Edna Mower still knits Double-rolled Mittens and socks, Beulah Moore hadn't knit a pair in 40 years when I met her. If you knit a pair, you will be helping to revive a nearly vanished craft, like making Clovis knife blades or writing hieroglyphs. They are special.

—R.H.

Double-rolled Mittens

Materials: 3 to 6 ounces worsted weight yarn, 1 to 3 ounces loose fleece or 1-inch pencil roving. The amount of yarn and fleece depends on the size.

Equipment: 1 set U.S. no. 2 (Can. no. 11) dp knitting needles, or size needed for you to knit the pattern to gauge.

Gauge: 6 sts = 1 inch in Double-rolled knitting.

Sizes: child's 2 to 3 years (child's 3 to 5, child's 6 to 8, child's 8 to 10, woman's medium, man's medium, man's large).

Pattern: The pattern comprises one st and the space between it and the next st. It's worked either by (1) flipping a thin, short roll of unspun fleece over the yarn between sts, always in the same direction so that inside the mitten the fleece appears to twine around the yarn; or (2) by knitting sts alternately over and under a strand of pencil roving or uncarded fleece. This creates a soft lining that, inside the mitten, looks like a yarn latticework over a fleece background.

Mrs. Moore suggests using loose fleece rather than

unspun carded yarn or products like Icelandic Lopi yarn. This is only necessary if one flips the yarn continually in the same direction. As every action has an equal and opposite reaction, after a round of flipping, the fragile, unspun wisp of fleece will be thoroughly spun—around the worsted. By using little bits, no more than 6 to 8 inches long, one can flip easier, and the end will go along for the ride without ensnaring the yarn.

One can use either loose fleece or split up bits of 1-inch roving. I confess that for my first Double-rolled Mitten, I had neither. Instead, I picked apart heavy Lopi yarn and recarded it, so that's a possibility, too.

If you start with raw fleece, and handle and wash the locks carefully, the fibers will stay nicely aligned, just as they came off the sheep. If not, and you're using loose fleece, you should use hand carders, those 4-by-8-inch rectangular tools spinners use that look like giant cat combs. If you don't know a spinner, or a place you can buy carders, you can write or call Halcyon Yarn, 12 School Street, Bath, ME 04530 for prices. Or, use two cat combs.

Card a handful of fleece until all the little fibers are lined up in the direction of the action. Then pick off a piece about ½ inch wide, pull it out about 6 inches long and rub it briefly between your hands to make it long and rounded, with the fibers still parallel. Make quite a few of these if you're taking your knitting with you somewhere. They can be kept in a plastic bag and are easier to carry than the carders.

If you're using 1-inch roving, break off a chunk about 3 inches long. Split it lengthwise into 4 equal parts and stretch each of these carefully to about 10 inches long. Roll each between your hands like a plasticene snake to give it some shape. A 10-inch piece is long; you can break it in two if you want, to make it easier to handle.

(1) Card a handful of fleece until fibers lie parallel.

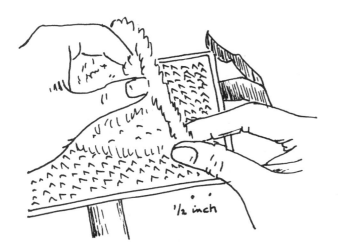

(2) Pick a strip about ½ inch wide off the hand carder.

(3) Pull it out smooth, to about 8 inches long, keeping fibers parallel as much as possible.

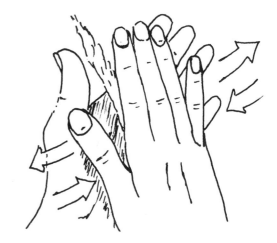

(4) Roll strip between your hands lightly.

To work the pattern: If you knit in the ordinary, old-time English way, you're in luck. Hold the roll of fleece up to the back of the st to be knit. Bring the yarn around the fleece as you bring the yarn to the needle to k. K the st as usual. The end of the fleece will be trapped in the space just before the st you just knit. Do this whenever you start a new piece of fleece.

(1) Lay the fleece across the yarn, close to the stitch just knitted, holding the long end down with the left index finger.

(2) Knit around it, anchoring the fleece.

Next st, and *all following*: With the knitting finger of your right hand, bring the long end of the fleece to the right, under the working end of the yarn. Flip it over the yarn and behind the next st. Hold it out of the way with your *left* index or middle finger, while you k one st with the yarn. Flip it over the yarn again for the next st, and so forth.

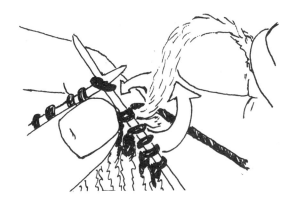

For American knitting: (1) Flip the long end toward you, under the yarn, then over it and away. Hold it in place behind the work with the left index finger.

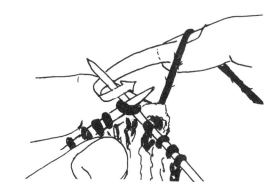

(2) Knit around the fleece.

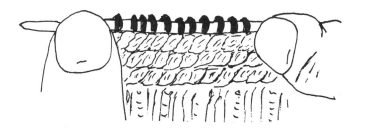

(3) Repeated with each stitch, the process produces a lining with this appearance, like Mrs. Brown's mittens.

If you knit in the Continental manner, picking the yarn off your left forefinger, this pattern will make you green with envy. We haven't found any way to do this technique quickly or easily using Continental knitting. You are welcome to try, but Continental knitting seems designed to keep things from getting twisted. You must alternate going over and under the fleece, although that doesn't really give the same density or the same neat look on the back side.

Under

over

(2) Knit one stitch over the fleece, the next stitch under it, lifting the fleece up and down to make this easier.

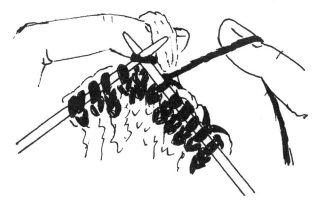

For both Continental knitting and Norwegian stranding, (1) carry the fleece behind your work, just as you would carry an unused strand in a contrasting color. In stranding, hold the bit of fleece on the left forefinger, the yarn on the right.

20

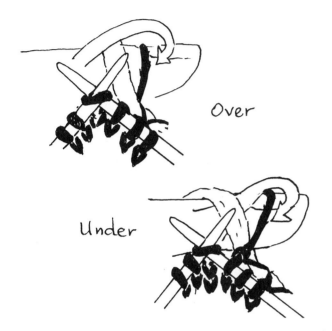

Over

Under

(3) In Continental knitting, hold the yarn on the tip of the left index finger, the fleece closer to the knuckle, then knit one stitch as usual, and go under the fleece to pick up the next stitch.

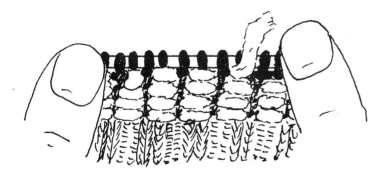

(4) This is the appearance of the lining created by the Continental and stranding methods—not as closely covered as in the English method, but still much warmer than ordinary mittens. Both Edna Mower and Beulah Moore use this method.

Cuff: With single strand of wool yarn and using the Maine method, cast on 30 (36, 42, 45, 48, 54, 60) sts. K 2, p 1 for 1¾ (2, 2, 2½, 2½, 3, 3) inches. (See General Instructions for Double-knitting for illustration of the Maine method of casting on.)

Change to pattern st and inc in first round once for thumb gore by knitting into the loop between the first 2 sts of the first needle. The base of the thumb gore will be these three sts. (Because the finished appearance of the mitten is striped, the increase used is one that emphasizes the vertical lines and makes them appear to branch off in Ys.) K pattern to end of round.

In the second round, continuing to double-roll after each st, k into the st directly under the st you would ordinarily k first (I'll call that, ''into the previous round''), then k the st directly above it. K 1, then k into the next st from the previous round, and k the st above it. You should now have 2 little Ys with the beginning of a vertical stripe between them. Inc in this way in the outside branch of the Y every second round until there are 9 (11, 13, 17, 19, 23, 25) sts in the thumb gore. K 4 more rounds. Put these sts on a string, and cast on 3 over the gap.

Hand: K straight up in pattern 2 (2¼, 2¾, 3½, 3¾, 4, 4½) inches.

Hand dec: At the beginning of each needle, k 1, k 2 together. At end of each needle, k 2 together. Dec this way every other round 2 (2, 2, 2, 3, 3, 3) times, then every round until 8 to 10 sts remain, depending on size. Break yarn, leaving an 8-inch tail. Using a yarn needle, draw up remaining sts with the tail and darn invisibly back and forth over the tip.

Thumb: Pick up from string 9 (11, 13, 17, 19, 23, 25)

sts on 2 needles. With a third needle, pick up and k 5 sts from corners and back of thumb hole. K straight up in pattern 1½ (1½, 1¾, 2, 2¼, 2½, 2¾) inches.

Thumb dec: K 1, k 2 together around twice. Break yarn, pull up remaining sts firmly on the tail, then darn back and forth across the tip.

Draw all tails into the mitten, turn it inside out, and darn the tails down securely. Trim off what's left.

Shag on cuffs: Shag is applied to ordinary knitting by stitching it into the fabric of the mitten in an overhand st around a spacer like a pen or pencil. The shag I've seen has not been knotted or even anchored by anything but the tension of the knit and the spreading of the cut ends of the yarn. It is an act of faith to cut such shag and expect it to stay in place, but neither of the examples I saw at the Maine State Museum had any bare patches, although one had been well used and the other was designed for work in the woods.

Thread onto a yarn needle a double strand of worsted weight yarn about 18 inches long. You will be stitching along the middle of a k rib, through the inward facing sides of 2 k sts. (If you hold the mitten cuff-down, these two sides will appear as an inverted V in the middle of the rib.) This puts the short, stubby bits of shag in the position of least tension, so they're not pulled loose by stretching the cuff in ordinary use. (If you stitch through the entire 2-stitch width of the rib, there will be an unattractive space between the 2 sides of the row of shag, and simply pulling the mitten on will stretch the cuff beyond the length of the shag and pull it loose.)

Lay a pencil or ballpoint pen along the rib and stitch over and over around it, going through 2 half

sts, one inverted V, each time. When you reach the hand portion of the mitten, stop and pull out the pencil. Don't clip the shag loops open until you've done all the ribs this way: the clipped ends tend to get caught in the working yarn.

When you're all finished, pull out the pencil for the last time, slip scissors through the lines of loops and clip them open. They will fuzz out to the sides and make a thick fur.

Shagged Loggers' Mittens

In 1903, John Richardson, of Mariaville, Maine, sheared his sheep, picked the tag ends out of the fleeces, and carefully washed the good wool. He took the clean fleeces to a mill—perhaps at Harmony, Phillips, or Caribou—where they were machine carded and wound into big rolls.

At home, his wife spun and plied the carded wool into a strong, creamy white yarn, still oily and smelling of sheep. John Richardson then knitted his sheeps' wool into socks and mittens and undergarments for his family.

Knitting hasn't always been a woman's job. I've come across a number of knitting men during my research, and historically in areas where knitting was a lucrative cottage industry, men have pitched in when not busy elsewhere. My own great-grandfather, a coastguardsman, knit socks and mittens for his family during long night watches at the Life Saving Station at South Cape May, New Jersey. Albert Miller's Special Hooked Mittens are the next pattern in this book. What I've seen of men's knitting seems always to have a strength and originality that separates it from women's.

We don't know what kind of socks or underclothes John Richardson knit, but a pair of his mittens was donated to the Maine State Museum in 1970 by his son's widow, who described in a letter her husband's recollections of how they were made.

John Richardson's mittens were knitted of natural, creamy, oily wool, and they were knitted a little smaller than the hand. When they were completely knitted and finished, he *sewed on* a thick layer of shag, stitching a double strand through the facing sides of two stitches, over and over a lead pencil, then cutting the loops into a pile as thick as an expensive wool carpet. Sewing two strands of yarn through every stitch forced the knit apart and

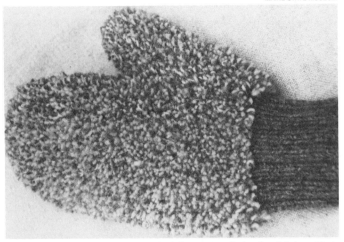

MAINE STATE MUSEUM

Shagged logger's mitten copied from a pair in the Maine State Museum made by John Richardson, of Mariaville, Maine, in 1903.

made the mitten larger, but also very tight against water, wind, cold—whatever winter had to offer.

"These mittens do not wet through as easily as common knit mittens," wrote Mrs. Nathan Richardson, whose husband received this pair from his father more than 80 years ago. When, at the Maine State Museum, we moved the pile apart to see how it was sewn, we could see little white places in the stitches and bits of pile; John Richardson had dyed the mittens black *after* he knit them. (I wonder now whether they were dyed in hot water, then cold, shrinking them some. Unless another such shagged-mitten maker is discovered, we will probably never know.) Today these mittens are still bright black and new looking, the cuffs unfrayed, the wool pile intact.

Shag mittens were not uncommon a century ago. Sturbridge Village has a number of pairs, so similar that one wonders if they weren't mass produced. The Nova Scotia Museum, in Halifax, has several pairs, and the Maine State Museum, in Augusta, has the granddaddy of all shagged mittens, a pair of sleigh driver's mittens with large hands and gauntlets extending to the elbows. (In the black-and-white photo, the upper mitten is shown inside-out.) As with Mr. Richardson's mittens, the shag is sewn in, but freehand, instead of following the lines of the knit. I will not even begin to tell you how to make them, as they are probably as useless today as they are splendid.

Shagged mittens were used mainly for driving, as their stiffness permitted little fine movement. They were designed to keep out the cold wind. John Richardson's were used in his woods, where he harvested bird's-eye maple, twitching the logs out with a span of big draft horses.

It was a little tricky figuring out instructions for Mr. Richardson's mittens, as the whole thing was covered with pile. Even inside, it was impossible to count stitches. Underneath, however, they seem to be ordinary, single-knit Maine mittens, similar to the fishermen's mittens, with a knit two, purl two cuff and marking purl stitches up the thumb gore.

Sturbridge Village Textile Curator Jane Nylander quoted from an 1830 woman's diary that said, "Shagged four mittens today." "It must not have been a job that took very much time," Jane remarked of the entry. I beg to differ. Why else did she mention it in her diary? It may have been her crowning achievement that day. Notice also that she specified "four" rather than saying "a couple" or not mentioning the number at all. I have shagged three-fourths of a mitten as I write this, and I tell you, it takes a little time and quiet space in one's life to shag a mitten. It's not unlike making a little rug.

—R.H.

MAINE STATE MUSEUM. PHOTO BY GREGORY HART.

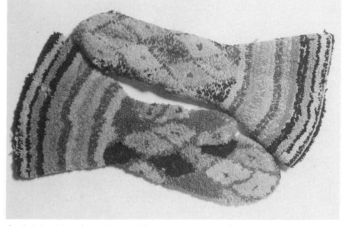

A sleigh driver's mitten with shag sewn in freehand.

Shagged Loggers' Mittens

Materials: For children's: 2 to 3 ounces wool yarn for mittens and 3 to 4 ounces yarn for shag. For adults': 3 to 5 ounces wool yarn for mittens and 6 to 8 ounces for shag. Shag and mitten needn't be the same color.

Equipment: 1 set U.S. no. 5 (Can. no. 8) dp knitting needles, or size you need to knit the correct tension. 1 set U.S. no. 3 (Can. no. 10) for ribbed cuffs. Yarn needle for finishing and shagging.

Gauge: 4½ sts = 1 inch before shag is applied.

Sizes: Child's 2 to 4 years (child's 6 to 8 years, adult's small, adult's medium, adult's large). These are the sizes *after* the shag is applied. Don't despair if they look a little small at first.

Pattern: The mittens are knitted in a plain k st on 4 needles.

Shag is applied after the mitten is finished, by laying a pencil along the vertical lines of the knit and with a yarn needle stitching through the side loops of 2 abutting sts, as shown, and drawing the yarn up around the pencil. If you're working from left to right, the next line of shag will be stitched through the other (right) half of one of these sts, along with the left half of a st in the next vertical line of sts.

The logic of stitching through the sides of 2 sts rather than through one st can be seen if you take the mitten and stretch it sideways. The space between the sts stretches less than the st itself, making it less likely that the short pieces of unanchored pile will slip out when the mitten is stretched in use.

Note how the spaces between stitches stretch less than the stitches themselves when the mitten fabric is pulled sideways.

Start stitching each line at the cuff and move the pencil up as you go, letting the lower end of the shagging slide off the pencil. Stitch as far up the mitten as that line of sts goes, then return to the cuff end and start over on the next line, holding the first row of stitching out of the way with one finger as you go.

When you've done 3 rows, slide one blade of a pair of scissors into the center roll of loops and clip them open. There's less problem with tangling if the line just before the one you are doing is not yet clipped.

Keep stitching and clipping until the whole mitten is covered. At times, the part already shagged will seem to be curling into itself almost too much, but remember, this isn't a carpet but a mitten, not meant to lie flat, so the curl means only that the mitten will be thick even where it curves around the hand.

It's easier if you clip any long ends at the end

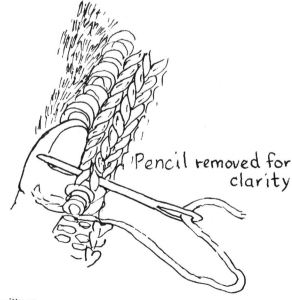

Pencil removed for clarity

Shagging mittens.

of each row to keep them from tangling into your work.

Some of the old mittens, like the Maine sleigh mittens, had flowers or other designs worked into the shag. This could be especially effective on a black or white mitten. If you want to do this, freehand embroider the design first, using the pencil as a spacer, then do the background along the lines of the knit—just as in needlepoint.

When it's all finished, including the thumb, even up the shag by holding the scissors sideways and clipping until it's smooth and wooly. Don't take off too much or the pile will pull free during use.

It might be a good idea to knit both mittens first and shag them afterwards.

Cuff: On the smaller needles, cast on 27 (30, 33, 36, 39) sts. K 2, p 1 for 2½ (2¾, 3, 3, 3½) inches.

Change to larger needles.

Inc for thumb: Move the last p st in the round to the first needle. P it, if you haven't already. Then k 1, k 1 into the loop between sts, k 1, p 1 (which should line up with a p st from the cuff).
K around. This is the beginning of the thumb gore. P these 2 sts each time and inc every fourth round within and next to these 2 marking sts 1 (2, 3, 4, 4) times until there are 5 (7, 9, 11, 11) sts between the p sts. K straight up, continuing the 2 lines of p sts until the thumb gore measures 1¾ (2, 2¼, 2¾, 3) inches, measured along the line of p sts. Put 5 (7, 9, 11, 11) thumb gore sts on a string, cast on 3 over the gap, and k straight up 2 (2½, 3, 4, 4½) inches for the hand.

Hand dec: K 2 together at both ends of all 3 needles every other round twice, then every round until 6 to 9 sts remain. Break yarn, leaving an 8-inch tail.

Using a yarn needle, draw up the remaining sts. Darn back and forth over the tip to strengthen it, then draw the tail inside and work it into the knit, following a row of sts for an inch or so. Trim the end.

Thumb: Pick up the 5 (7, 9, 11, 11) sts from the thumb gore on 2 needles. With a third needle, pick up and k 5 sts from the back and corners of the thumb hole. K straight up for 1 (1¼, 1½, 1¾, 2) inches.

Thumb dec: K 2, k 2 together in the first round, then k 1, k 2 together until only about 6 sts remain. Break yarn and finish as on the hand.

Now, using pattern instructions above, cover the entire mitten, thumb and all, except the cuff, with shag.

Mittens Hooked on a Dowel

I wanted to bring Maine folk mittens to the Washburn-Norlands Annual Heritage Days, to show them to people, but the person I called there told me it wasn't necessary.

"We have our own kind of mittens up here—and a man who hooks them," she said.

Wild horses couldn't have kept me away.

He was in his seventies and sat at a card table, talking across a display of his mittens and a couple of those reels mounted with baby food jars that some people think are a convenient way to store nails or spices.

He was making a mitten, quickly, deftly, using a funny little hook that was sharp on one end but otherwise resembled a crochet hook. I watched. The mittens on the table were clearly synthetic ("Wool wears out too fast," he told me later, smiling. "This is warmer than wool."), but were they thick! And solid!

When he finished that mitten, the second, he opened a little notebook and wrote "257" under "256." It was his 257th pair that year, he said. It was June.

I asked him to show me how, but he said I needed a cuff first. He himself had a boxful of paired cuffs ready to work on, behind the table. I hurried back to my display to knit a cuff.

Albert Miller comes from central Maine, and was for years a schoolteacher in one-room schoolhouses, accustomed to applying discipline firmly where it was needed.

He learned to make "hooked" mittens from his mother, who brought the little-known technique with her when she emigrated from Poland. He'd been making them off and on as a hobby for 70

Mittens Hooked on a Dowel. Albert Miller made the dark pair. The front mitten is worked with one-, two-, and three-round stripes to show possibilities.

years, and until recently had kept the method a secret. In the past five or six years, however, he changed his mind and decided it would be better to teach people the technique—which he thought his mother had invented—in hopes that it would be carried on.

Albert had a set of instructions printed up and began making more hooks. He had more cuffs knitted. "You can't do this with a crochet hook," his son, Lowell, told me, and he's right. I've tried.

At one workshop at the Livermore Falls Senior Citizens Center, he expected two or three people to show up. No fewer than 63 men and women came to learn to make Albert's wonderful mittens, and Albert managed to teach them all. One

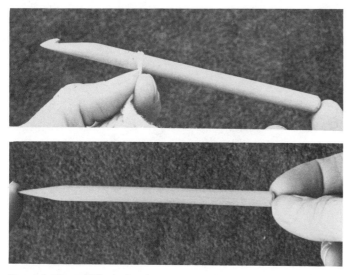

One of Albert Miller's hooks, made from a birch dowel, about 5 inches long.

man completed his first mitten before he left that evening.

For years one could get a set of instructions and a handmade hook by sending him a dollar-fifty. "I have to charge that," he explained, "because it takes time to make them."

Albert Miller died in the winter of 1984–85, but Lowell, who can also hook mittens but is less busy at it, gave me permission to share the technique in this book. He also gave Merrill's of Maine, a wooden knitting needle and crochet hook factory, permission to make and sell the hooks.

"He would have wanted it that way," Lowell assured me.

—R.H.

Mittens
Hooked on a Dowel

Materials: 3 to 5 ounces worsted weight wool yarn (for example, Briggs & Little 2/8 or Bartlettyarns Homespun). Mr. Miller always used a sturdy worsted weight *synthetic* yarn, and vowed that wool neither held up as well nor was as warm. Although I don't agree with him about the warmth, there are many people in central Maine who wouldn't use anything but synthetic yarn for these mittens. It's up to you.

Optional: Small amounts of contrasting or harmonizing colors for stripes.

Equipment: Hooking Dowell from Merrill's of Maine, West Street, Kennebunkport, ME 04046. Mr. Miller made three sizes: a large one for people who crochet tightly, a small one for those who work loosely, and one for medium people like me. Compare your crocheting with a couple of crochet patterns and see how you come out before you order.

You will also need 1 set U.S. no. 4 (Can. no. 9) dp knitting needles, or size needed to k 1, p 1 at a tension of 6½ sts per inch. Yarn needle for finishing.

Gauge: 6 sts = 1 inch in slip-stitch crochet worked through the front of the st only.

Sizes: Small (about child's 8 to 10), medium (woman's medium), and large (a little bigger than man's medium, but not as large as my size man's large in other patterns).

Pattern: Called *potad* mittens in rural Sweden, these are called "special hooked mittens" by Albert

Miller. Everyone who makes them objects to their being called crocheted mittens. This may be because they are much denser than most crocheted mittens, which one expects to be full of little holes. These mittens have no little holes anywhere, and done in steel wool could probably repel enemy bullets.

The mittens are worked in a crocheted slip-stitch through the front loop of each st in the preceding round. To make the work easy (or even possible), you must have the kind of sharp, flattened needle Albert Miller's mother used, and must push the needle deeply into each new loop as it is formed. This regulates the tension and makes a loop the needle can get into in the next round.

To dec: Poke the needle through two sts from the preceding round, make a slip st, pulling it to the usual tension. To inc: Slip-stitch twice into the same loop of the preceding round.

If you have difficulty counting rounds on the outside of the mitten, count on the inside, where the rounds are clearly marked.

Albert Miller demonstrated his method of making mittens to many groups in his last years and sold hooks he made of birch dowels, as well as a typewritten set of instructions. These instructions are reproduced here with only such additions as he made when teaching in person.

Cuff: Cast on 38 (40, 42) sts, dividing them among 3 dp knitting needles. K 1, p 1 for 3 inches. Bind off loosely.

Place a safety pin vertically through the sts in the cuff directly above the beginning of the round. Place another smaller safety pin into the cuff vertically in the sts exactly opposite the beginning of the round. These are inc and dec points.

Hand: Hook 2 rounds, hooking into every st of the cuff in the first round.

Add a st above each marker in rounds 3, 5, 7, and 9.

Hook a total of 10 rounds before taking off for the thumb. In the eleventh round, beginning at the small marker, hook through both sides of the st, then hook a chain of 6 (8, 10) sts, skipping 8 sts in the preceding round. Fasten this down by hooking through both front and back loops of the ninth st in the preceding round. This forms a slot for the thumb. Hook around as usual. Remove the small marker pin.

Hand dec: Hook 7 rounds and dec 1 st at the marker. This and the following decs will make the mitten curve in on the little-finger side, just as your hand does. Hook 6 rounds and dec 1 st at the marker. Hook 5 rounds and dec 1 st at the marker. In the next 6 rounds, dec 1 st every other round.

Make your mitten to the end of the index finger. If it's not long enough already, continue for as many rounds as you need to, but dec 1 st above the marker every round. If the mitten's already longer than the end of the index finger, pull it out to that point and continue from there.

In the next round, begin a general dec. For large size: dec 1 st in every 7. In the next round, for large and medium size, dec 1 st in every 6; in the following round, for all sizes, dec 1 st in every 5. Reduce the number of sts between decs by 1 st in each round until at last you are decreasing in every st. When only 7 or 8 sts remain, break the yarn, pull the tail through the last st, and thread it onto a yarn needle. Catch up all the remaining sts on the tail and pull them up tight. Then darn the end into the inside surface of the mitten, turning it inside out to do so.

Thumb: Pick up 5 more sts than double your chain, 17 (21, 25) sts, adding 3 of these sts on the inside (palm side) corner of the thumb hole and 2 on the outside (knuckle side) corner. (Mr. Miller thought mittens with even a tiny hole on the palm side of the thumb were no good. In general, he had no use for any of my mittens because of this and because they were made of wool.)

Hook 3 rounds with the same number of sts, then dec 1 st on the palm side in the fourth and fifth rounds. Continue straight to the end of the thumb, for a total of 2 (2½, 3) inches.

Dec every other st for 2 rounds. Then dec every st for one round. Break yarn, thread it through the last st, then onto a yarn needle. Pick up the remaining sts and draw them up tight. Darn the tail, and all other tails, into the inside surface.

Shag on the Inside: A Mystery Mitten from Massachusetts

Erin Pender, of Hampden, New Hampshire, wrote me about these special mittens in response to my request for information about fleece mittens in an article in *Down East Magazine*. "I know what fleece mittens are," she wrote. "These mittens were in Lowell, Mass., the winter of '54 or '55. I had borrowed them from a playmate for the afternoon. They were the warmest mittens I've ever worn, before or since. They were multicolored, as if the knitter had snippets of various colors of worsted weight yarn such as are used for markers, and had knitted them in with the mitten so that the tails were inside to create warm 'fleece.'"

Mrs. Pender checked back with her now grown-up playmate, and her friend's mother, but the mother didn't remember the mitten, and the friend didn't know where the mittens had come from, whether from a local person or from someone of recent European extraction, only that her mother had given them to her. Mittens matching this description, but with loops rather than ends inside, are knit in Sweden (*100 Landskapsvantar*, 1982) and in eastern Europe, perhaps Latvia (Leszner, 1982).

I tried to make a mitten based on Mrs. Pender's description, but like the European women, I didn't dare cut the loops to make an inside shag. And surprisingly, it didn't matter, because the loops don't catch fingers after all. Just don't try to pull on the mittens over a ring with a fancy setting.

I took my inside-shag mitten to Mrs. Pender in New Hampshire, and she said it wasn't quite right, that there should be no bumps on the outside. The mitten she remembered was multicolored, perhaps in ombre yarn, with cut snippets rather than loops on the inside and no sign of them on the outside. She also thought the snippets might have been knotted in.

A mitten shagged on the inside, based on a description by Erin Pender and comparison with similar European mittens.

So there you have it. With a firm basis in European tradition but little more than a rumor to support it in this country, this pair of mittens is at best marginally a New England folk mitten. But it's warm and squashy and funny looking, and it uses up scraps. Maybe it will become a folk mitten.

—R.H.

Shag on the Inside

Materials: 3 to 6 ounces worsted weight wool yarn. 2 ounces varicolored scraps, each at least 4 inches long. For the mitten shown, I used scraps of Persian wool crewel embroidery yarn that had been sitting around for years waiting for my interest in embroidery to revive. (Of course, I ran out of real scraps and had to go buy more.) You needn't be so lavish unless you want to be. Presumably, this pattern is designed to use up scraps thriftily.

Equipment: 1 set U.S. no. 4 (Can. no. 9) dp knitting needles, or size needed to obtain correct gauge. Yarn needle for finishing.

Gauge: 4½ sts = 1 inch, on round with yarn scraps knitted in.

Sizes: Child's size 2 to 4 years (child's 6 to 8, adult's small, adult's medium, adult's large). These sizes allow extra space inside for the shag.

Pattern: A multiple of 2 sts and 4 rounds. The scraps were k in every second st of every second round as shown in the graph. Because I had no access to the person who originally made these mittens, I had to experiment, and wound up with this.

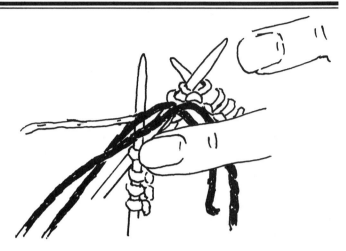

(1) Knit one round in stockinette, working the thumb gore stitches according to instructions. In the second round, knit one stitch. Before knitting the next stitch, hold the end of the scrap yarn (two strands of worsted weight yarn, or four of lighter yarns) against the back of the knit with the third finger of the left hand, leaving a one- to two-inch tail pointing down. Do this each time you start a new scrap.

Cuff: On dp needles, and using Maine method, cast on 33 (36, 39, 45, 48) sts. See General Instructions for Double-knitting to learn the Maine method of casting on. K 2, p 1 for 2½ (2¾, 3, 3½, 3½) inches.

Change to stockinette st and begin pattern. Also in the first round, begin inc: In the first needle of the first round, k 1, k 1 into the loop between the first and second sts, k 1, p 1. K around to the last st and p it. The 2 p sts mark the edges of the thumb gore. Inc 1 st within and next to these marking sts in each succeeding fourth round, maintaining the line of p sts.

Beginning in this first inc round, work the pattern.

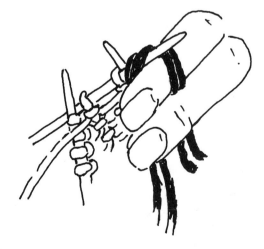

(2) Wrap the long part of the scrap yarn around the left index finger and over the needle as if to knit. Hold the (long) end out of the way behind the knit with the left index finger. This forms a loop.

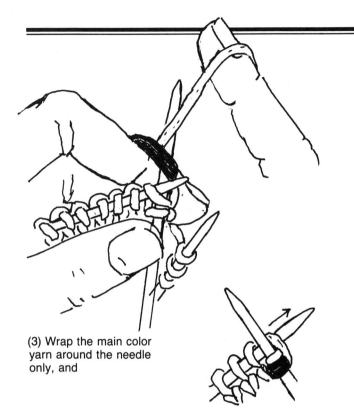

(3) Wrap the main color yarn around the needle only, and

(4) knit both together. Remove the left index finger from its loop, and knit one more stitch in stockinette. Repeat the pattern every second stitch every other round, shifting over one stitch in each pattern round as shown in the graph. On the next round, knit each contrasting strand together with the stitch immediately following, thus locking the contrasting yarn in place.

(It seems to be impossible to work a loop into the p sts; instead, just catch up the scrap yarn by purling over it and knitting the next st under it.)

Inc a total of 3 (4, 4, 5, 5) times for 9 (11, 11, 13, 13) k sts between the p sts on the thumb gore. K without increasing until thumb gore measures about 2 (2¼, 2¼, 3, 3) inches from the cuff, measured along the line of p sts.

Put the 9 (11, 11, 13, 13) thumb gore sts on a string. Cast on 3 sts over the gap. K straight up (stop knitting p sts) 1½ (2½, 2½, 3, 3½) inches for the hand.

Hand dec: The first 3 sts on the first needle are directly above the 3 sts bridging the thumb hole. You will dec on both sides of them, and on both sides of the three sts exactly across from them, in the middle of the second needle.

On the first needle, dec: K 1, slip 1, k 1, pass slipped st over k st. (This procedure is called psso in most knitting books.) K to 1 st before middle 3 sts of second needle; k 2 together, k 2, slip 1, k 1, pass the slipped st over the k st and k to the last 2 sts on the third needle; k 2 together.

Dec this way every second round. When 16 to 20 sts (depending on size) remain, divide sts equally between 2 needles with all the palm sts on one needle and all the back sts on the other. Try to get a last round of loops in here if you can. Graft the 2 sides together, sewing from one side to the other with a yarn needle in imitation of a row of stockinette st.

Thumb: Pick up from string 9 (11, 11, 13, 13) sts, 1 st from each side of thumb hole, and 3 sts from the top. Total 14 (16, 16, 19, 19) sts. K straight up 1¼ (1½, 1¾, 2, 2¼) inches in pattern. Dec sharply: K 1, k 2 together for 2 or 3 rounds, still in pattern, until only 6 to 8 sts remain. Break yarn, draw up remaining sts on the tail firmly, and darn the tail into the end of the thumb.

For this pattern only, carefully work the ends of the worsted yarn into the outside surface of the mitten, following strands that are part of the knit. Turn the mitten inside out and snip off any longish ends of the shag.

Now, for a pleasant surprise, slip on this mitten from Massachusetts. Then knit another.

Wristers

You probably know these handcoverings from the movies more than from real life, unless you're from Europe or England. Ebenezer Scrooge wore them in *A Christmas Carol,* and everyone wore them in *Dr. Zhivago* when there was no indoor heat. They're the abbreviated indoor mitten, the mitten that lets you work too, but because American and Canadian houses are usually warm enough we tend to think of them as something worn only by poor people in the movies or as something foreign.

They are also called "fingerless gloves" and "pulse warmers," which explains both their shape and their function. For some reason, if the wrist and palm are kept warm, the body will maintain the fingers *gratis* in mild cold. Mainers call them wristers, Canadians call them "mittens," and in a recent fashion magazine, I saw them called "mitts," which is what most Canadians and Englishmen call what Americans call mittens, if you get the picture. To bring the terminology full circle, some Newfoundlanders call what we're calling mittens "cuffs."

Nowadays, in Maine and Maritime Canada, they're used mostly by fishermen to protect their wrists from chafing by their freezing oilskins, but not very long ago, they were worn throughout the area under larger mittens that had no cuffs at all.

My first pair came from Phyllis Wharton at Seal Harbor. They arrived one day in January—white, wooly, smelling of sheep, a real fisherman knit. I tried them immediately, and as the temperature in our house was about sixty as usual, I kept them on for most of the winter. They are marvelously functional in today's America of turned-back thermostats, and are useful for such outdoor occupations as delivering newspapers and ice-fishing.

The red and blue pair is my own combination of the double-knitting and wrister traditions, knitted for my 11-year-old son, who was going camping one particularly cold weekend in early February. They have a thumb gore like an ordinary mitten, but they fit tighter, more like a glove. The top edge is six rounds of ribbing to keep it from curling.

Another kind of wrister is the All-cuff Wrister. Barbara H.P. Wells, who grew up in Maine but now lives in Coraopolis, Pennsylvania, wrote me, "My mother kept us well supplied with fancy mittens, but we made our own wristers, also of wool. We used 2 needles—k 2, p 2 (of a number divisible by 4). They reached 'a good way' up our arms and covered our hands to the middle knuckle of our longest finger. We left a (2- to 3-inch) opening for our thumbs when we stitched up the seam. We were ready for anything in those lovely cold Maine winters."

To make the All-cuff Wrister, start with worsted weight yarn, 2 U.S. no. 4 (Can. no. 9) needles, and cast on 32, 36, or 40 sts (for sizes very small, medium, and large enough). Most children over four years old and most women will fit the 36-stitch size nicely. Then follow Mrs. Wells' instructions. These are very fashionable in New England in 1985, and girls—oddly enough—wear them *over* their mittens or gloves. If you want to do that, use the next size larger. But remember that you will be creating a nice pocket for snow between the layers.

If you would like to make fishermen's wristers like Mrs. Wharton's, consult the first wristers pattern given in my book *Fox & Geese & Fences* (Down East, 1983).

—R.H.

Salt and Pepper Wristers

Materials: 1½ ounces each lt and dk worsted weight (such as Briggs & Little 2/12) wool yarn. The example was worked in Brunswick Yarns Germantown.

Equipment: 1 set U.S. no. 5 (Can. no. 8) dp knitting needles, or size needed to knit correct gauge. 1 set U.S. no. 3 (Can. no. 10) for ribbed portions. Yarn needle for finishing.

Gauge: 6 sts = 1 inch in Salt and Pepper.

Sizes: Instructions are for small size to fit children from 4 to 6 years old. Instructions for medium (which seems to fit everyone from medium-sized children to women's medium) and large (men's medium and large) are in parentheses.

Pattern: I chose Salt and Pepper for this because it's one of the simplest patterns in appearance and because it is a very smooth, flat pattern that can be worn under a large mitten out-of-doors, and that won't hamper finger movement when worn alone indoors.

Salt and Pepper, a multiple of 2 sts worked on an

uneven number of sts, can be knitted flat, but is best worked round for these instructions.

Be sure to read General Instructions for Double-knitting before starting this project.

Cuff: Cast on 32 (36, 40) sts in dk yarn on smaller needles. K 2, p 1 straight up at least 3 inches or up to 4 inches. Put in stripes in lt if you wish after 8 rounds. Change to larger needles and Salt and Pepper pattern, and inc 1 st in the first needle to make an uneven number of sts by knitting both colors into one st.

Start thumb gore: At the beginning of the second round, k both colors, in the right order, into 2 consecutive sts. Mark the outside of this inc with a bit of contrasting yarn between the new fourth and fifth sts if you think you'll have trouble seeing it. Inc this way, 2 sts each side of the thumb gore, on every fourth round 3 (4, 5) more times, then k straight up in pattern until thumb gore measures 2½ (3½, 4½) inches. Put 11 (15, 19) thumb gore sts on a string, cast on 5 (7, 9) sts over the gap and k up in pattern 4 (6, 8) more rounds, or as long as you want to. The base of the fingers is a good place to stop, if the hand you're knitting for is available to try it on.

Change back to the smaller needles and k 2, p 1 in dk for 6 to 8 rounds. Bind off rather firmly. The edge should be elastic but should not hang loosely or curl back.

With the smaller needles, pick up the 11 (15, 19) sts from the thumb gore, and 7 (9, 11) from the back and corners of the thumb hole. K 2, p 1 straight up for as many rounds as the top edge on the hand. If this seems too loose, and it may, pull out the thumb and reknit, knitting 2 k sts together at both corners in the first round. The ribbing won't be

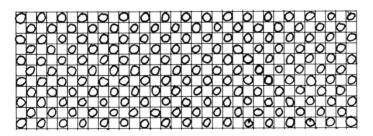

quite right any more (there will be 2 places where it will be k 1, p 1) but it's only for a few rounds and it won't show much. You may want to dec this way once more on the inside of the thumb before you bind off. Wristers usually fit rather closely, like gloves.

Bind off just as for the hand, break yarn, and darn all ends into the inside surface of the fabric.

The second wrister is identical to the first because there is no difference between the back and the palm.

Part Two
Double-knit Mittens and Gloves

Double-knit Mittens and Gloves

The beautiful designs on these mittens and gloves are not our patterns, nor are they new. They come from men and women in New England and Atlantic Canada who learned them by sitting next to a friend or a mother or an aunt, and watching her knit. They learned the little peculiarities of increasing and decreasing that go with that mitten, learned the stories associated with it: how it came into the family, what its colorful name means in relation to its geometric design.

In other words, these patterns are as much folklore as songs like "Springfield Mountain" and "Calico Bush," as much folk art as quilt patterns. In fact, many of them parallel quilt patterns.

The people they come from are the early settlers of the coast: the French, the English, Scots, Channel Islanders, Irish, and the Norwegians. Those who came later—the Finns, the Italians and Portuguese, the Russians, and others—seem to have dropped their own knitting traditions in favor of local ones or simply gone over to purchased mittens. A year-long inquiry in the Maine Finnish community produced not one Finnish mitten, although Finland certainly has knitting traditions distinct from the rest of Scandinavia.

These patterns all have ties to Europe and the British Isles—often surprising ones. Many of the more esoteric qualities of the mittens knit by old Yankee families showed up in a book on double-knit mittens from the island of Gotland, in Sweden. Some of the Newfoundland/Labrador patterns are known in Estonia, although Estonian immigration may not have been noteworthy in Labrador. A star pattern that looks Scandinavian appeared from a woman of English/German descent, who said it was British.

This doesn't mean that English settlers picked up knitting traditions from Gotland on their way to Maine, or that someone from Estonia settled in Newfoundland and set up a knitting school for young girls. Instead, it reflects the seagoing tradition of earlier centuries, the trade and codfishing links between all the north Atlantic communities. Mittens are not a drawing room tradition; they come from plain, hardworking people—fishermen, woodsmen, and farmers.

If women in Maine and Gotland knit the same mitten, it's because a once-widespread pattern has survived in these two places. Because no one ever told these knitters that stockinette cuffs were no longer *de rigueur* in mitten fashions, they continued to knit them and pass them down, while knitters in other more trafficked areas invented another kind of cuff (ribbed) and passed the idea around.

The British Isles and Scandinavia have a rich tradition of fishermen's and farmers' sweaters. Not so North America. What seems to have survived of the old knitting traditions here is found in smaller garments like mittens, socks, gloves, and caps, possibly because the handmade item is so superior to anything available commercially.

Those presented here and in Robin's first book, *Fox & Geese & Fences*, and in Janetta's booklet, *Nova Scotian Double-Knitting Patterns*, are only some of the double-knit patterns in New England and Atlantic Canada. There are perhaps half as many again as there are knitters—other patterns, endless combinations of patterns, other stories.

These are a few that we liked. Some are widespread, still actively knitted. Others are on the verge of extinction. But all of them fit well into today's northern life and fashion.

General Instructions for Double-knitting

For those who knit in only one color, knitting with two or even three colors must seem an esoteric skill living only in hands born to it. Perhaps Norwegian women have the skill in their genes and need only to have it awakened at age six or seven to be wonderful knitters.

To the single-color knitters of the world, I say that nobody in my family double-knit anything, although all the women and little girls could knit, fast and smoothly, without mistakes. We loved Scandinavian sweaters, Norwegian mittens, Fair Isle sweaters, but it never occurred to us that we could knit them ourselves. And if it had, reasonable instruction in the art simply didn't exist until recently.

We were told everywhere to pick up the new color from underneath (Did "new color" mean the contrast color or just the color about to be used?) with the result that the two yarns steadily and inevitably became twisted around each other and had to be untwisted every few rounds—a bore at best. The result of this questionable method is a lumpy piece of knitting with an indistinct pattern.

I would like everyone to know that jacquard, or double, knitting is not something present in the genes of the elect, and that it can be learned and done with skill by anyone who wants to do it. I am living proof of this.

The fabric needn't be lumpy or strangely pulled up, and it can come off the needles perfectly flat, with even tension, and a back side as neat as the front.

The first axiom is: *never twist the yarn*. (And its explanation, like unto it: don't pick up both colors the same way.)

Carrying the Main Color Ahead

Pick up one color, the background color, usually the lighter one, from above (or to the right of) the other. Pick up the second, contrasting color (often the darker one) from beneath (or to the left of) the main color. The contrast color will stand out slightly on the right side of the knit but it will do so consistently. And it will look good.

On the back of the fabric, the background color will dominate, and there will be straight lines as regular and neat as the design on the front.

In Maine and eastern Canada, this technique is called "carrying the dark color ahead," because the dark strand is picked up from underneath and *ahead*— in the direction of knitting—of the light strand. The light strand is always brought around (and above) the dark. From the knitter's viewpoint the light strand seems to be slipping around from behind when it's picked up.

Knitters familiar with both right-handed, Anglo-American knitting and left-handed Continental knitting can use both with two colors: hold the dark strand on the left forefinger and the light on the right. This is called "stranding" and is associated with Norwegian knitting. Knit the dark strand the Continental way, the light the American way. The yarns can't get tangled, and the dark will be "carried ahead." When I use this method, the patterns that are meant to be ridgy flatten out. I like to have the contrast color standing out a bit, so I don't use this method.

Knitters in the Continental tradition, who pick the yarn off their left forefinger with the knitting

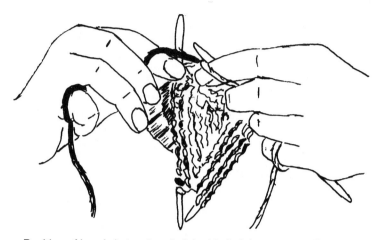

Position of hands in two-handed double-knitting, or stranding. Knit the left-hand yarn the Continental way, the right-hand yarn the American way.

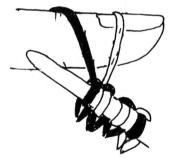

Continental double-knitting, position of dark and light strands. The strand nearest the knuckle is the one emphasized on front of work.

needle, should place the contrast color in the crease of the left forefinger, the background color nearer the fingertip. Pick both of these the same way and don't go under either to get to the other, except if there are many stitches between color changes. (See "Weaving In," below.)

Some Anglo-American knitters catch up the dark yarn with their forefinger from in front of the light yarn and the lighter yarn from behind with the middle finger. Look closely at the drawings to sort out this rather inexpressible idea.

In all these methods, tension is controlled by holding the yarns in the third and fourth fingers, or by twisting the yarns around these fingers.

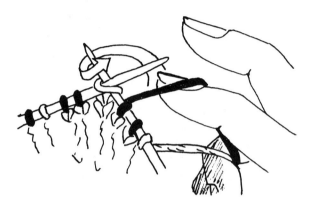

(1) American right-handed double-knitting. Knit the dark strand. Then, to change colors—

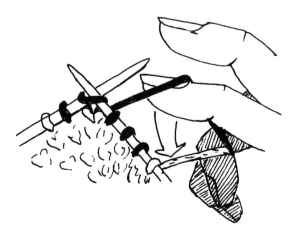

(2) catch the light strand on the underside of the index finger.

40

(3) Change fingers,

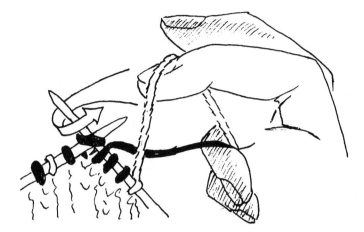

(5) Knit the light strand. Then, to change colors—

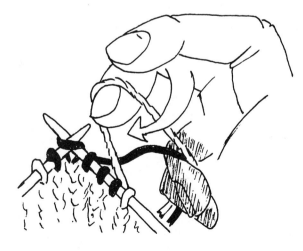

(4) then catch the light strand on the back of the index finger.

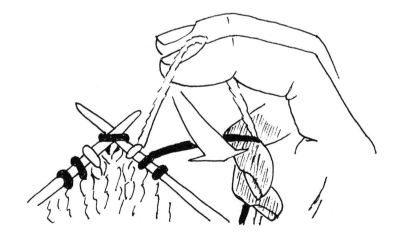

(6) take the light strand between the middle and index fingers and bring it over the dark strand.

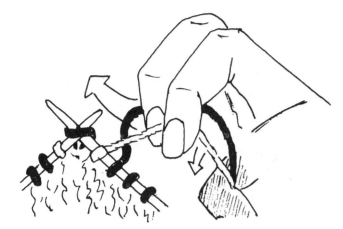

(7) Catch the dark strand on the back of the middle finger,

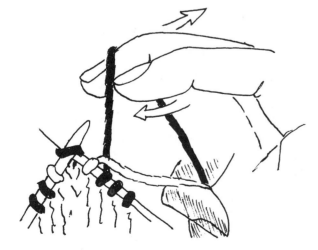

(8) shift it to the index finger,

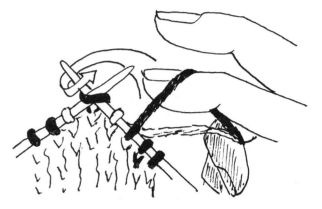

(9) and knit the dark strand.

Gauge

The second axiom of double-knitting is: *be sure to check the tension in the pattern you're using.* Some of the patterns—for example, Chipman's Block, Stripes, and Peek-a-boo—are meant to pull up slightly (or even a lot) into ridges. These must be knit on larger needles to get the same gauge as other patterns.

Janetta and I found that even if we knit the same number of stitches per inch horizontally, we knit a different number of rounds per inch vertically. Because of this possible difference, all the vertical measurements here are given in inches, although traditionally the measurements are given in bands, as "Knit three bands for the wrist, three for the thumb gore and five for the hand."

Increasing for the Thumb

Mittens would be simple if it weren't for the thumb. The thumb makes the hand wider where it begins at the wrist, then wider and wider until it separates from the hand, leaving a gathered group of four fingers. This makes mittens not so simple.

Ways of coping with the thumb: (left to right) a New Sweden, Maine, mitten with all the increases in the first two rounds above the cuff; a Maine fisherman's mitten with a triangular thumb gore marked by purl stitches; a Norwegian-style mitt from Newfoundland with a triangular thumb gore marked by two contrasting lines and a different pattern; a Maine Compass mitten with all the increases in one (light) round; a Newfoundland mitt with typical palm, triangular thumb gore, and white marking lines; a Nova Scotian mitten has a triangular thumb gore with no outline; an Acadian mitten with no thumb gore but more stitches around the hand to accommodate the thumb.

We have used several methods of increasing for the thumb, all of them taken from traditional knitters. Where and how they are used differs from region to region, mitten to mitten, and knitter to knitter.

Newfoundland mitts, for example, are knitted all on one size needles. This means there must not only be an increase for the thumb, but also for the hand itself, as the hand portion shouldn't cling as closely as the cuff. At the top of the ribbed cuff, a stitch is added between some or all of the two knit stitches in each rib by picking up the loop between stitches as if it were another stitch and knitting

it. This increases the total number of stitches by either one-third or one-half depending on whether there are two or three knit stitches in every rib to knit between.

Increasing at top of cuff. Knit as usual. Second stitch from right and second stitch from left are increases.

Some mittens have no thumb gore at all and rely on a heavy increase like this at the top of the cuff to provide room for the thumb, but most of the mittens in this book have what is vaguely referred to as a triangular thumb gore, even if it winds up looking a lot more like a top-heavy parallelogram.

Moving up the thumb gore of the Newfoundland mitts, stitches are added on the thumb gore side of two contrasting vertical marking lines by knitting both colors into one stitch.

Increasing by knitting both colors into one stitch.

In Maine and parts of Nova Scotia and New Brunswick, it's common to add a whole pattern element at a time on the thumb gore. As the whole mitten is knitted in the same pattern, this affects the shape of the mitten so much that it's almost impossible to transfer instructions for one pattern to

43

another, as one can with Newfoundland/Labrador and Norwegian-style mittens, which usually change only the pattern on the back of the hand.

These all-over patterns are usually transmitted in terms of blocks, or bands ("Knit up two blocks, then add one block . . .") and are heavily dependent on the number of stitches in the particular pattern element. In a pattern based on a multiple of eight, for example, eight new stitches would be added, in one round, in the space of eight stitches, in the center of the thumb gore. Sometimes knitters use a different, smaller pattern for the thumb and thumb gore just to avoid increasing so many stitches in so little space.

To increase this way, use a combination of two methods: knitting both colors into the same stitch and looping the yarn between stitches as if to knit. When increases and stitches are this closely packed, increasing by looping the yarn doesn't leave a hole, but beware of it in other situations.

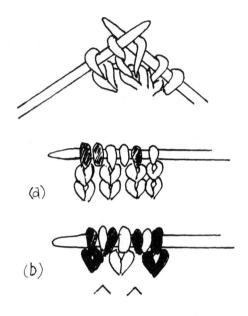

Increasing by knitting into the back of the stitch from the previous round, then knitting the stitch above, as usual: (a) with one strand, (b) with two strands.

Increasing by knitting both colors into one stitch and looping as if to knit.

On other mittens from this region, particularly those like Stripes and Double-rolled Mittens with strong vertical lines, increase by knitting into the back of the stitch *below* the next stitch with either one or both strands, depending on the pattern, then knitting the stitch above it as usual. Done in the dominant color, this makes the dark line appear to split in two with a light stitch in between.

Most of the Nova Scotian and New Brunswick patterns here call for an increase of one stitch each side of the thumb gore with no marking line of contrasting stitches. The increase is made by knitting both colors into one stitch, as in the Newfoundland/Labrador mitts. The thumb gore and the hand are mentally separated into two units, each with the same pattern, the one on the thumb gore growing outward by two stitches every second round. Sanity is maintained by using a yarn marker carried on the needle.

I didn't find this method easy and avoided it on all but Fleur-de-lis and Diamonds, where the diagonal lines seemed to preclude any other method.

Decreasing

As with increases, so also with decreases: everyone has his own way.

The women in Labrador/Newfoundland tend to decrease at both sides of a mitt, two stitches to a side, every round, almost to the tip. At this point the Norwegian Newfies part company with the Anglo-Celtic Newfies and keep ploddingly decreasing just as before until they reach a point with one or two stitches on each needle. The tip of the finished mitten is like a housetop, what Maine knitters with a sniff call a ''picked'' (as in ''picket'' fence) tip. The other Newfoundland/Labrador knitters either begin decreasing in the center front and back when ''pickedness'' threatens or graft the last 16 to 20 stitches to make a rounded tip.

Further south, knitters are also divided. An old tradition exists of decreasing by whole pattern elements, knitting two stitches together on as many consecutive stitches as are needed to eat up a single element (12 stitches for a six-stitch element), or to decrease the pattern element itself, if that works well, by taking stitches off each element.

The knitters who use these two methods for decreasing also tend to increase by whole pattern elements on the thumb gore.

Both give a rounded mitten tip that maintains the integrity of the pattern all around. They're very organic endings for a mitten.

A third old method, used both on single-colored and double-knit mittens, is to decrease by knitting two stitches together at both ends of all three needles every round. This too makes a nice rounded tip. The method varies from pattern to pattern, some calling for two decreases at both

Different ways to end a mitten: (clockwise from top) a Maine mitten decreased at both ends of all three needles; a Maine mitten decreased by dropping whole pattern elements in single rounds (by knitting two together as many times as there are stitches in the pattern element); a Nova Scotian mitt decreased at both edges, then grafted across the blunt tip; a Norwegian-style pointed finish (decrease two each side all the way to a point); a Maine mitten decreased all the way around by knitting two together between pattern elements (and by eliminating whole pattern elements).

ends of each needle every two rounds, others demanding an odd order for the knitting together that maintains the integrity of the pattern.

All three methods produce an ambidextrous mitten that can be worn on either hand or trained to one.

There is a modern tradition, however, of decreasing by two stitches on each side of the mitten, at first every other round, then every round, and finally grafting the last 20 or so stitches together to make a rounded or slightly squared-off tip. This method ignores what happens to the pattern at the two decrease points, but since hands usually show only their backs or their palms at one time, the decrease lines don't show much. As this kind of decrease makes a mitten distinctly a left or right, one must be careful to make only one for each hand per pair!

In the grafting method as well as the Newfoundland/Labrador one, decreases must slant toward the tip. This is easy enough on the far end of the needle, where knitting two stitches together does this naturally, but it's not as easy at the beginning of the needle, where we twist the two stitches to be knitted together. To avoid this twist and get a decrease that slants in the right direction, use a method of that famous knitter Barbara Walker: slip the first stitch as if to purl, onto the right needle. Slip the second stitch as if to purl. (Elizabeth Zimmerman, another famous knitter, recommends slipping the second stitch as if to knit. Either works.) You now have two stitches backwards on your right needle. Now put them back on the left needle as they are and knit through the back of both stitches.

Weaving In

If the pattern you're about to knit has distances between color changes no greater than three stitches, don't bother reading this now. It's too distressing and complicated, and I wrote a whole book on double knitting before I learned about weaving in, so you can live without it a few days longer too.

I generally consider weaving in a nasty thing to do to a piece of double-knitting, because it often shows on the right side and detracts from the finished appearance, but sometimes it's necessary.

Weaving in means that the yarn-not-in-use is caught up between stitches with a half-twist around the yarn-in-use. It's necessary when color changes take place more than three stitches apart, to prevent long loops inside the mitten that might catch on a finger and pull loose, later breaking and destroying both the pattern and the mitten.

Janetta likes to weave in any "leap" of more than two stitches. This makes her knitting flatter and denser than mine and seems to pull it tighter in the vertical direction.

I only weave in on leaps of five or more stitches, weaving in on both sides of stitch number 3 on a leap of five and stitch number 4 on a leap of seven or more. Some Canadian-Norwegian mittens I have seen have leaps as long as 12 stitches with no weavings-in at all, but this seems a little foolhardy.

I personally feel that few patterns are worth having to deal with frequent leaps of more than five stitches by weaving in the background yarn. However, some seemingly tiny patterns have these five-stitch leaps: Double Irish Chain and Partridge Feet both have a five-stitch leap in every element, and I wouldn't lose them for anything. On the other hand, Big Waves has mile-long leaps I'm willing to put up with to get its spectacular effect. But it's not my everyday pattern.

Each knitting method has its own method for weaving in, and as usual, it's the Anglo-American right-handed knitter who has to work the hardest.

For Contintental knitting: To weave in the light strand (near the fingertip) while knitting the dark strand: Go over, then under the light strand to pick up the dark. Knit it. If the positions of the yarns change when you do this, so that the light strand now lies closer to the knuckle, go under it to get to the dark strand for the next stitch. If not, just pick up the dark strand as usual. This catches up the light strand twice, twisting them once, but untwisting them in the next stitch.

To weave in the dark strand when knitting the light, reverse the procedure: Dig under the dark strand to get to the light. Knit the stitch. In the next stitch, go over the dark to get to the light yarn. This undoes the twist.

For the two-handed stranding method: To weave in the left strand, insert the needle in the next stitch, then lift the left strand so it rests on the right needle in the opposite direction from the direction the stitch will be in. Knit the right strand as usual. Then drop the left strand back where it belongs to knit the next stitch. This will undo the twist.

To weave in the right strand while knitting the left, insert the needle in the next stitch, then bring the right strand under the right needle and hold it on the left side of the needle above the left strand while you knit the left strand in the usual way. Bring the right strand back where it belongs and knit the next stitch. You will find the right strand fastened to the back of the fabric by two twists of the other color.

For Anglo-American knitting: Pick up the color you wish to weave in from the "wrong" position; that is, go through the motions of changing colors, but

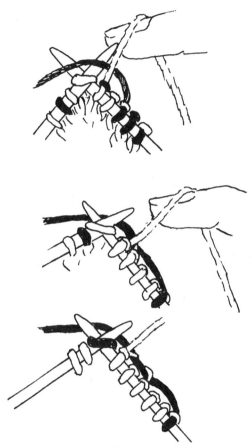

Weaving in, two-handed stranding method.

pick up the dark yarn from above (or behind), the light from beneath or ahead. Doing this will give them a half twist in the process. For the next stitch, however, you'll have to unwind this; go through the yarn changing motions again, but pick up the yarn to be knit from its usual position, untwisting the two yarns in the process. Understand? If not, consult the drawings on changing colors in this old-fashioned knitting method (in the earlier section on "Carrying the Main Color Ahead"). It's not hard once you do it a few times.

Casting On

Every knitter has a favorite way of casting on stitches at the beginning of a project. I assume that you can knit and that you know how to cast on, too.

However, I offer an old-fashioned cast-on shown to me by Nora Johnson, a traditional knitter from Five Islands, Maine, because it gives a firm, slightly elastic, and tight edge. It's useful for any mittens (sweaters and socks, too!) but it's essential to mittens with stockinette cuffs, as it keeps them from curling at the edge. For this bit of instruction, refer to the following series of drawings, which are worth at least a thousand words, I assure you. This method is called the ''Maine method'' in the directions.

(A flexible alternative, used for some of the Nova Scotian mittens in this book, is to cast on in any method but using needles one or two sizes larger than those used for the ribbing. This is *not* recommended for double-knit cuffs in stockinette stripes or the Peek-a-boo pattern.)

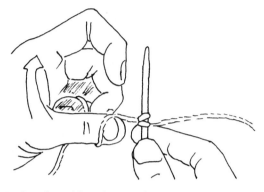

(2) Rotate thumb and hand upward.

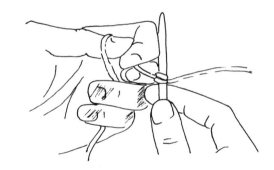

(3)

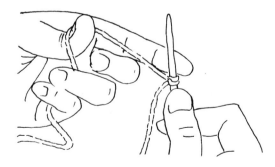

Maine Method of Casting On. (1) This is the third stitch. To begin, follow the same steps but omit the needle until the sixth step shown here.

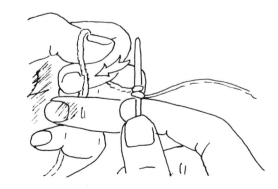

(4)

(5) Slip thumb out and turn index finger away, like a make-believe pistol.

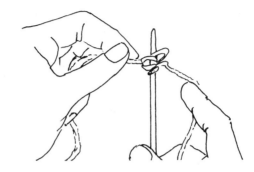

(8) Slip finger out and pull up stitch.

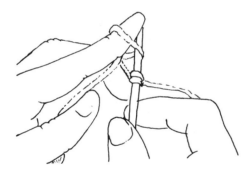

(6) Insert needle into loop on index finger as if to knit.

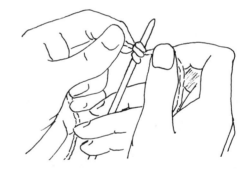

(9) Pull up tight on both sides.

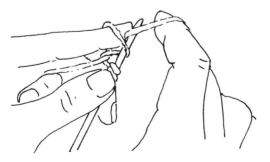

(7) Knit, using left index finger as if it were the left needle.

Cuffs

In northeastern North America, cuffs come in several forms.

Cuffs at one time were a separate unit not even attached to the mittens. In Maine, these were called wristers. These were made of a harmonizing color, or gray, in a knit two, purl one, or knit two, purl two rib and were slipped on before the mitten. One woman told me she remembered as a child wearing wristers to her elbows over her winter jacket but under her mittens.

Cuffs nowadays are knit two ways, and they are usually part of the mitten. There is the ordinary ribbed cuff, sometimes striped (to even out yarn consumption) and almost invariably in a knit two, purl one, or knit three, purl one, rib. I have seen only one traditional knitter in the area who makes a knit two, purl two ribbed cuff. The consensus is that knit two, purl one, or knit three, purl one, makes a more elastic cuff. Some knitters say they don't have to change needle sizes when they reach the main body of the mitten if they use one of these two combinations. (Mr. Miller's dowel-hooked mittens have the only knit one, purl one, cuffs I've seen in the area.)

The other kind of cuff is in stockinette stitch! Yarn is cast on in one color, using the Maine Method

A variety of cuffs.

shown above. (These cuffs are made only in Maine and various British islands, to my knowledge.) A two-color pattern is begun in the next round, either knit two dark, knit two light, or knit one light, knit one dark, or Peek-a-boo (see Cunnin' Old-timey Baby Mittens). As all three of these patterns tend to pull up the fabric in ridges and make a closer tension than what usually follows, they function somewhat as ribbing on cuffs. At least the first two, with their vertical stripes, even look a little like ribbing.

Mittens with these cuffs look marvelously hand-made and old-timey.

Sometimes the pattern on the rest of the mitten is also knit on the cuff. Although such cuffs look loose, they generally fit quite snugly and don't let in any weather at all. They are, of course, double-knit and hence warmer than a ribbed cuff. I wouldn't knit a cuff like these on any of the Newfoundland/Labrador mittens, but on the small geometric patterns from farther south, they look great.

—R.H.

Double-knits with British Roots

Most of the double-knit mittens in Maine, Nova Scotia, and New Brunswick are knitted in small, all-over geometric patterns that come from families of primarily Yankee/Scots-Irish/Scottish/English descent. They have been on this continent a long time. No one knows for sure where they came from, but some are knitted in the British Isles today in much the same way they are knitted here.

Some Mainers attribute certain patterns to acquaintances from the Maritimes or Nova Scotia. Some Canadians are sure the patterns came to them from the States with the Loyalists and other immigrants. In fact, there has been so much backing and forthing between the Maritimes and New England, and so many shared attributes between the two areas that the mingled traditions will probably never be sorted out. And it probably doesn't matter.

Janetta has written most of this section, because she was collecting patterns in Nova Scotia and New Brunswick long before it ever occurred to me, and she knows more about the knitting in those two provinces than I ever will.

Of the patterns here, graphs of Flying Geese, Northern Star, and Mattie Owl's Patch first appeared in her book, *Nova Scotian Double-Knitting Patterns*, recently published in an expanded form by the Nova Scotia Museum.

I've put in a word or two concerning patterns that also occur in Maine or that I know something about, but really, this section belongs to Janetta.

—R.H.

Janetta Dexter.

Flying Geese Gloves

Flying Geese pattern on gloves.

This pattern was shown to me by Mrs. Murdock Hollingsworth, of Truro, Nova Scotia, in 1974. She told me it was traditionally used for gloves, with four bands of pattern on the back of the hand and carried up to the ends of the fingers. A fifth band is carried the length of the thumb.

With the yarn ordinarily used for double-knitting in Nova Scotia, this made much too large a glove. I could reproduce it only by using a very fine yarn (Lady Galt Kroy) and Can. no. 14 (U.S. no. 0) needles. I have so far knit them only in one width, although the length of the fingers can easily be adjusted. One way to widen the pattern would be to knit two one-stitch lines of white separated by a single-stitch dark line separating the pattern elements, rather than having them separated by a single-stitch white line.

This glove pattern is certainly not for beginners, but a careful, experienced knitter can create a masterpiece.

The pattern itself is very simple to knit and can be used with coarser, worsted weight yarn for mittens or hunter's mitts, with three bands of pattern each on the back and the palm.

I usually use white or light gray for the geese against a navy blue, black, or dark gray background.

—J.D.

Anyone who lives along the flight routes of the geese knows the thrill of hearing their honking in the fall and the early spring as they pass overhead in long **V** formations. Besides knitting patterns, there are quilt patterns, Pueblo Indian pottery designs, and Navaho rug designs named ''Flying Geese,'' reflecting the empathy that we earthbound feel for the large birds in their cooperative flights north and south.

—R.H.

Flying Geese Gloves

Materials: 2 ounces (500 grams) each lt and dk, fingering weight or fine sportweight yarn. Lady Galt Kroy by Paton and Baldwin, or Brunswick Yarns Pomfret both work well for these gloves. They are traditionally worked with a navy blue, black, or dk gray background with lt gray or white geese.

Equipment: 1 set Can. no. 14 (U.S. no. 0) dp knitting needles for the cuffs. 1 set Can. no. 12 (U.S. no. 2) dp knitting needles, or size needed to knit pattern to gauge. Yarn needle for finishing.

Gauge: 9 sts = 1 inch in Flying Geese pattern. Check your gauge before you start by knitting a little tubular swatch, or check it after you've knit about an inch. But be sure to check it, and don't cheat, or your Flying Geese gloves won't be what they should be—a masterpiece of needlecraft. It's easier to rip out an inch than to fall into despondency when the first glove comes out too large or too small.

Sizes: Man's medium only.

Patterns: Flying Geese (or Diving Geese variant) and Salt and Pepper.

Both variants of the Flying Geese pattern are a multiple of 10 sts plus 1. Flying Geese has a four-round repeat; the Diving Geese variant, a six-round repeat.

First round: K 1 lt, k 4 dk.

Second round: K 1 lt, k 3 dk, k 1 lt, k 1 dk, k 1 lt, k 3 dk.

Third round: K 1 lt, k 2 dk, k 2 lt, k 1 dk, k 2 lt, k 2 dk.

Fourth round: K 1 lt, k 1 dk, k 3 lt, k 1 dk, k 3 lt, k 1 dk.

For the Diving Geese variant, k the first 4 rounds above, then continue for two more rounds.

Fifth round: K 1 lt, k 1 dk, k 2 lt, k 1 dk, k 1 lt, k 1 dk, k 2 lt, k 1 dk, around.

Sixth round: K 1 lt, k 1 dk, k 1 lt, k 2 dk, k 1 lt, k 2 dk, k 1 lt, k 1 dk, around.

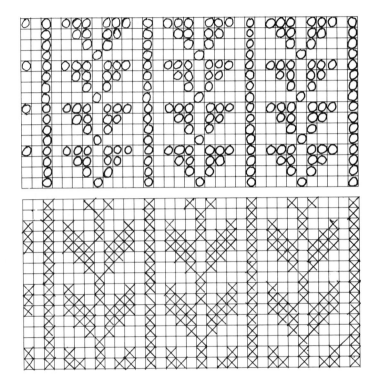

Top: four-round Flying Geese pattern. Bottom: six-round Diving Geese variant.

(Since the geese are knitted just on the backs of the gloves, you must add one more lt st to the last pattern element in each round to finish the design.)

Salt and Pepper, used for the palm side of the gloves, is a multiple of 2 sts and 2 rounds. This two-st alternation is the simplest bicolored pattern there is. In Maine, whole mittens are done in Salt and Pepper, simplified even more by knitting it on an uneven number of sts, so that the alternation changes itself every round. In Atlantic Canada it's used as a filling design where a larger pattern is difficult to fit into a space.

First round: K 1 dk, k 1 lt, around.

Second round: K 1 lt, k 1 dk, around.

Be sure to read General Instructions for Double-knitting before starting this project.

Cuff: On larger needles, using dk yarn, cast on 72 sts, 24 sts on each needle. K off onto smaller needles in k 2, p 1 ribbing. Continue ribbing for 3 inches.

Begin pattern and change to larger needles. In the first pattern round, inc 4 sts on each needle. Total: 84 sts on 3 needles.

Left glove: Begin knitting in Flying Geese pattern on the first needle. On the second needle, continue Flying Geese pattern to the middle of the needle, ending the fourth block of pattern with the extra lt st. K the remaining sts on this needle in Salt and Pepper pattern. On the third needle, k in Salt and Pepper to within 4 sts of end. Then, k 1 lt, k 3 dk to form the base of the back side of the thumb gusset.

Increasing for the thumb gusset is a bit tricky, as Salt and Pepper and the Flying Geese patterns have different methods of increasing. Set things up after the first round by slipping the first lt st of the first needle (the first lt st of the Flying Geese pattern) onto the third needle. Now put a marker between the ninth and tenth sts from the end of the round on the third needle.

K 2 more rounds.

Inc in the fourth round. About 4 sts from the end of the Salt and Pepper portion—just after the marker— inc: K both colors, lt then dk, into each of (any) 2 adjoining sts in the Salt and Pepper portion. Inc this way in the Salt and Pepper portion every fourth round twice more.

In the Flying Geese portion (the last 5 sts on the third needle), k both colors into the first lt st, lt then dk, k across in dk, then k both colors, dk then lt, into the final lt st. Inc this way every fourth round twice more.

You will add 4 new sts in each inc round, for a total of 12 new sts.

After the second set of incs (the eighth round) you can begin a 1-st lt vertical stripe in the center of the dk sts of the thumb gusset. This will become the centerpoint of the pattern when you reach the third set of incs.

When you have increased 3 times, there should be a total of 21 sts between the marker and the end of the third needle.

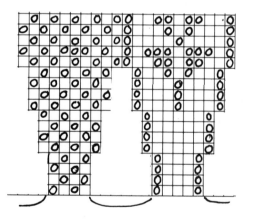

Detail of thumb gusset increases.

When 5 ranks of Flying Geese, or 3½ ranks of Diving Geese, are completed, place the last 21 sts from the third needle unto a string for the thumb.

Cast on 9 sts across the gap and continue in pattern for 4 more ranks of Flying Geese (2 bands plus 4 rounds in Diving Geese).

Take off for the little finger: K up to 11 sts before the center of second needle. Place 22 sts on a string for the little finger. Cast on 6 sts over the gap and k 2 rounds, maintaining the pattern.

Take off for the ring finger: K up to 12 sts from the center of the second needle; place 24 sts on a string for the ring finger. Cast on 6 sts and k 1 round.

Take off for middle finger: K up to 13 sts from center of round and put 26 sts on a string for the middle finger. Cast on 6 sts over the gap.

Adjust remaining 30 sts on 3 needles. K forefinger with one Flying Geese pattern on the back and the remainder in Salt and Pepper. K straight up for 2¾ inches, or to end of finger when glove is tried on. Then dec: Slip 1, k 1, pass the slipped st over the knitted st at the beginning of each needle. At the end of each needle, k 2 together, until 6 sts remain. Maintain patterns. Break yarn and pull up these 6 sts on both strands.

Middle finger: Pick up 6 sts along lower edge of forefinger, being careful not to leave holes at the corners. Place these and the sts from the string for middle finger unto 3 needles. K middle finger (3 inches, or to tip of finger), carrying Flying Geese pattern up the back and Salt and Pepper on the remainder. Finish just as for forefinger.

Work third (2¾ inches) and fourth (2½ inches) fingers the same way, picking up 6 sts from beside the preceding finger each time.

Thumb: With one needle, pick up 11 sts at corners and along back of thumb hole. Put the 21 sts from the string on the other 2 needles, and k thumb to required length (2½ inches, or to tip). Dec and close off in the same way as for the other fingers.

Draw all tails to the inside of the glove and darn them into the inside surface.

The right glove is k just as the left, except that the first 7 sts on the first needle form the beginning of the thumb gusset, and you k 3 dk, k 1 lt *before* beginning to work in Salt and Pepper on this needle in the first pattern round.

Flying Geese pattern on mittens.

Partridge, or Crow's Feet, Mittens

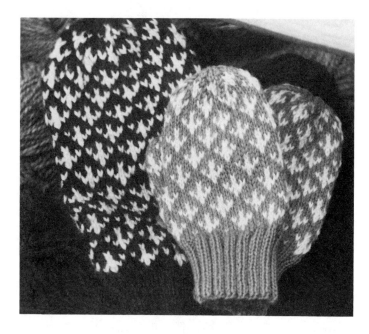

A friend of mine at Yankee Yarns in Brunswick, Maine, first told me about Partridge mittens. "Wait'll you see Partridge Mittens," she said when we were deep in a mitten discussion one day. "You'll love them!" I waited and watched, but I never saw a partridge, mitten or otherwise. I saw lots of other mittens and so I imagined what a partridge mitten would be like and knitted a little swatch with hen tracks following one another in a straight line like partridge tracks in the snow.

I showed it to my friend, and she said no, that wasn't right. "Well, show me! What's wrong about it?" I demanded.

"Well, I can't tell you. It's just not right."

"But I can't find a Partridge Mitten!"

"You will. Someday," she said unhelpfully.

Although someday hasn't come, and I still haven't found a real live Partridge Mitten made by a traditional knitter, Pat Flaherty sent a little graph of a chicken foot and a sketch of a Partridge Mitten, which she called Crow's Feet. The only problem was, she gave me no return address, and so I was unable to write back to her.

She said—and others have said—that Crow's Feet is knitted around Blue Hill, Maine. Others have told me the Searsport Yarn Shop published a pattern for Crow's Feet Mittens, but people at the shop say they didn't.

And so, here is the much-sought-after Crow's Feet—or Partridge—Mitten. It is a very flexible and comfortable mitten, especially when made with a soft wool yarn. It has no ridges and no lumps, and if you catch up the loops on one particular round in the pattern, there will be nothing to catch your fingers in either. Be sure to carry the contrasting (light) color ahead this one time.

—R.H.

Partridge Feet Mittens

Materials: 2 to 3 ounces each dk and lt colored worsted weight wool yarn (Briggs & Little 2/12 will do). If the cuff is not striped, about 1 ounce more of the main color.

Equipment: 1 set U.S. no. 3 (Can. no. 10) dp knitting needles, or size needed to knit pattern to gauge. 1 set U.S. no. 2 (Can. no. 12 or 13) for ribbed cuff.

Gauge: 7 sts = 1 inch in Partridge Feet pattern.

Sizes: Child's 4 to 6 (woman's small, woman's medium, man's medium). Other sizes don't readily fit the pattern.

Pattern: A multiple of 8 sts and 8 rounds. This pattern can be knit flat for caps and sweaters, but be sure to add an extra st at both ends for the seam.

First round: K 1 lt, k 3 dk, k 1 lt, k 3 dk, and repeat around.

Second round: K 2 lt, *k 5 dk, k 3 lt* and repeat * to * around.

Third round: K 1 lt, k 1 dk, k 1 lt, k 3 dk, k 1 lt, k 1 dk, and repeat around.

Fourth round: K 1 lt, k 7 dk. Repeat around.

Fifth round: K 1 lt, k 3 dk. Repeat around.

Sixth round: K 3 dk, *k 3 lt, k 5 dk*. Repeat * to * around.

Seventh round: K 2 dk, *k 1 lt, k 1 dk, k 1 lt, k 1 dk, k 3 lt*. Repeat * to * around.

Eighth round: K 4 dk, *k 1 lt, k 7 dk*. Repeat * to * around.

Note: Catch the lt yarn up on the stretches of 5 or 7 dk sts.

If you want to make a Maine-style snug cuff, use a 4-st-wide vertically striped pattern (k 2 dk, k 2 lt) in stockinette st, using the larger needles. You won't need the smaller needles at all.

Be sure to read General Instructions for Double-knitting before starting this project.

Cuff: On smaller needles and using dk yarn, cast on 40 (48, 52, 60) sts. K 3, p 1 for 2 (2½, 3, 3) inches.

(OR, for a snug Maine cuff, use the larger needles only and cast on, using the Maine method, the same number of sts as above. Then k 2 dk, k 2 lt, etc.)

Change to larger needles and begin pattern, adding 0 (0, 4, 4) to make a multiple of 8 sts. In the same round, mark the thumb gore.

Thumb gore: For the right mitten, the first 8 sts of the round (for the left, the last 8 sts of the round) will be the base of the thumb gore. Please put a marker between the eighth and ninth sts, as it's easy to lose your place in this pattern.

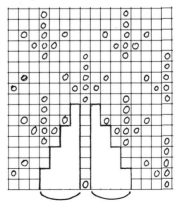

Thumb increase detail.

Inc in the third round of pattern. Study the graph of the thumb detail first: the right edge of the graph should correspond with the beginning of the round; the left edge with the end of the round. The incs are placed to happen in the background color without affecting the footprints.

Inc whenever possible within the limits of the pattern by knitting both colors into 1 st. When this is not possible, k into the loop between sts on both sides of the center st. If there's a need to catch up the background yarn in the first few rounds, do so just before and just after increasing.

There will be an especially long distance between lt sts in the fourth round (9 sts), but be calm, and catch the lt yarn up at least twice behind your work, and everything will be fine.

Inc every 2 rounds, following the graph until there are 16 sts on the thumb gore. Wherever possible, inc by knitting both colors into the sts on either side of the center st. Try to keep the little feet looking as clean and undistorted as possible.

For man's medium continue to inc until there are 24 sts between the marker and the end of the needle.

K straight up until 1½ (2, 2½, 2½) inches above the cuff.

Take off for thumb: Put on a string 15 (15, 15, 23) sts, grouped around the center st of the incs. Cast on 7 sts over the gap and k straight up 2½ (3, 3½, 3½) inches.

Hand dec: On the fifth round of a foot (the round with k 1 lt, k 3 dk), k 2 dk sts together just before and just after the lt st beginning each new foot.

Next round (sixth of pattern): K 2 together dk once between each 2 feet.

Next round (seventh of pattern): K 2 together twice on the 4 sts between the center toes of each 2 feet. In the next round, k 1 lt, k 2 together dk around. If more than 16 sts remain, k 2 together around in dk, breaking lt yarn with a 6-inch tail and stuffing it inside the mitten. Continue to k 2 together dk until 12 to 16 sts remain.

Break yarn, draw the remaining sts up on the dk tail, and darn back and forth across the tip. Draw both tails into the mitten through the tip.

Thumb: Pick up from string on 2 needles the 15 (15, 15, 23) sts from the thumb gore. With third needle, pick up and k in pattern 9 sts from back and corners of the thumb hole. (The pattern will be upside down on these sts from the rest of the hand, so base what you do on where you are on the visible part of the thumb, not on what's happening on the palm side.)

K straight up in pattern for 1½ (2, 2¼, 2¼) inches, or just to the tip of the thumb, if you have the right person's thumb handy. Decrease and end just as you did on the hand.

Finish: Draw all tails to the inside, turn mitten inside out, and darn tails securely into the inside surface. Turn it right side out and it's ready to wear.

Northern Star, or Maplewood, Mittens

I found this old pattern framed in the small museum at Maplewood, Lunenburg County, Nova Scotia. I later learned that it was a piece of a Larrigan sock, the huge, double-knit socks men used to wear under the moccasinlike Larrigan boots, and over their heavy wool work pants.

I called the pattern by its place of origin for some time before I found out that its rightful name is Northern Star. If you look at the pattern you can see two stars—a dark one with a dark diamond in its center and a light one with a light diamond in its center. It's an optical illusion of the sort craftswomen love to play with.

—J.D.

Quilters who see this pattern always exclaim, "Rob Peter to pay Paul!" Any patchwork pattern that uses the leftover parts of one square to make up its opposite in the next square is named with this colorful expression, which sprang up when a church tax in the Middle Ages was diverted from the building of St. Peter's Cathedral to the building of St. Paul's. It's almost a pity we can't apply the name to this pattern, but although it seems to burst forth spontaneously from the lips of quilters, it really doesn't belong to knitting.

When I first saw this pattern at Janetta's house, she had knitted it into a mitten, dark blue and bright blue, as in the example. I loved it immediately, but when I asked her to knit a sample for this book, she knitted in dark navy blue and light sheep's gray. The sharp contrast in colors changed its appearance entirely, emphasizing all the little bits and pieces, and it was hard to see the design at all. Because Northern Star is a "busy" pattern, it looks best knitted in two fairly close colors like dark gray and light gray, dark blue and light blue, or maybe dark red and a heathery red.

—R.H.

Northern Star Mittens

Materials: 2 to 3 ounces lt and 2 to 3 ounces dk worsted weight wool yarn, preferably different shades of the same color.

Equipment: 1 set Can. no. 11 (U.S. no. 2) dp knitting needles, or whatever size you need to knit pattern to gauge. 1 set Can. no. 13 (U.S. no. 1) dp knitting needles for ribbed cuff. Yarn needle for finishing.

Gauge: 7 sts = 1 inch in Northern Star pattern.

Sizes: Child's size 4 to 6 years (child's 8 to 10, woman's medium, man's medium, man's large).

Pattern: With a multiple of 10 rounds (two 5-round bands) and 14 sts (two 7-st blocks), Northern Star is awkward for some sizes and impossible for very small mittens unless worked in finer yarn.

To ease the awkwardness, we've included logical answers that other knitters have surely thought of before. On sizes where there's an odd number of 7-st blocks (every other size), the "extra" block necessarily has to adjoin an identical pattern block. Janetta arranges the pattern so that one of these blocks is on the palm, the other on the back, so it doesn't show much. She catches up the background yarn on the inside to avoid finger-catching loops.

Robin splits the odd block in two and runs this split block up the thumb gore and then up the palm to the forefinger; this makes the pattern work. We've included a graph of a split block to help you out. Please note that it has 8 rather than 7 sts. Add the extra st at the center of the block by knitting both colors into 1 st, as you need it.

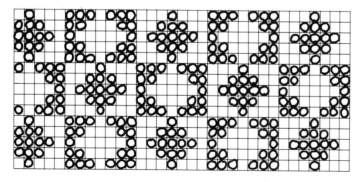

Be sure to read General Instructions for Double-knitting before starting this project.

Cuff: On the larger needles and with dk yarn, cast on 36 (45, 51, 57, 63) sts. K off unto the smaller needles in k 2, p 1 ribbing. K 2, p 1 straight up for 2 (2½, 3, 3, 3½) inches, striping if desired with lt yarn.

Change to the larger needles and stockinette st. Begin pattern, increasing 6 (5, 5, 6, 7) sts *evenly spaced*, in the first round. This gives a multiple of 14 sts in child's size 4 to 6, woman's medium, and man's large. For child's 8 to 10 and man's medium, you must use one of the ruses offered under "Pattern" above, as you will have one 7-st block too many (or too few!).

The first 7 sts on the right mitten and the last 7 sts on the left mitten form the base of the thumb gusset.

Inc for the thumb gusset: In the sixth round, add enough sts above the thumb gusset block to make another 7-st block. Inc by a combination of knitting both colors into single sts and by looping the yarn as if to k between sts, but maintain the pattern as you go.

The number you inc will vary from 6 to 8 depending on whether you're going from an even number of blocks to an odd number of blocks (with a split block of 8 sts) or going from an odd number of blocks (with a split block of 8 sts) to an even number of 7-st blocks. Splitting a block makes perfect sense when you're doing it, but it's very complex to put in writing. You may think that it would be better not to do this pattern at all rather than deal with split blocks and such, but I assure you, the resultant mitten is worth the effort.

At the first round of the next band of pattern, inc this way again only for the men's sizes, and put the split block, if there is one, on the palm side of the thumb gusset.

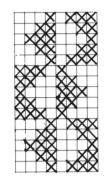

Split pattern blocks.

When you've knit 2 (3, 3, 3½, 4) 5-round bands up from the cuff, put on a string 14 (13, 14, 20, 20) thumb gusset sts, cast on 6 (7, 6, 6, 6) sts over the gap in pattern. Put the split block in the new sts on child's sizes 8 to 10 and men's medium only. The others should come out even.

Hand: K straight up in pattern for 4 (4½, 5, 5½, 6) 5-round bands.

Beginning on the first needle, dec: Slip the first st, k 1, pass the slipped st over the knitted st. K up to 2 sts from the middle of the second needle, then k 2 together, slip 1, k 1, pass the slipped st over the knitted st. K up to 2 sts from the end of the third needle. K these 2 sts together.

Narrow every other round this way 2 (2, 3, 4, 4) times, then every round until 16 (18, 20, 24, 26) sts remain. Divide these sts equally unto two needles, one each for the palm and the back sts, and graft across the end, looping between front and back sts with a yarn needle in imitation of a row of stockinette st.

Thumb: Pick up and k unto one needle, in pattern, 8 (9, 8, 8, 8) sts from the corners and back of thumb hole. For the 3 smaller sizes, you will have a split

block on the thumb. Put it right here, coming up from the back of the thumb hole.

Pick up and k 14 (13, 14, 20, 20) sts from the string unto the other 2 needles, carefully matching the pattern so it's exactly right on the side that shows. K straight up on these 22 (22, 22, 28, 28) sts for 1½ (2, 2¼, 2¼, 2½) inches.

Thumb dec: Look at where you are in the pattern. It's nice if you can end up with the sides of the square and the tip of the diamond coming together at the tip of the thumb, creating the look of a little flower or a pinwheel on the end. Get this look by decs *within* the color: where there are more than one st of a given color, k 2 together until you're down to about 6 to 8 sts.

Break the yarn, pull the dark strand through the remaining sts and draw up firmly, then darn back and forth across the tip.

Draw all the other tails to the inside of the mitten, turn it inside out and darn them all to the inside of the fabric. Trim the ends.

Turn it right side out and it's ready to wear.

Compass Mittens, or Mattie Owl's Patch

in that pattern every since, calling it Mattie Owl's Patch.

The pattern is not limited to the Cruikshank family, however, or even to Nova Scotia Indians. Other families in the Sherbrooke area knit it and call it Noughts and Crosses. I learned that folkcraft writer Joleen Gordon found it knitted in the Barrington, Nova Scotia area, where it is called Compass Work, and a woman in New Brunswick sent it to me under the name Spider's Web.

It seems to be an eight-stitch variant of Fox and Geese* (which is six stitches square).

—J.D.

My distant cousin Bertha York, of Harpswell, Maine, has childhood memories of her aunt knitting this pattern, which they called Compass Mittens, or Compass Work. To my knowledge, this pattern is no longer passed from hand to hand in Maine.

—R.H.

This pattern has many names. I first learned of it from Mrs. Viette Cruikshank in Liscomb, Guysborough County (Nova Scotia). Mattie Owl, an Indian woman, called one evening many years ago at the home of Mrs. Cruikshank's grandmother. Mattie Owl was wearing a ragged pair of double-knit mittens which had been patched with scraps from other handknits, and the Liscomb woman's eye was caught by the double-knit pattern on the patches—this pattern.

She gave Mattie Owl a pair of new double-knit mittens then and there in trade for the ragged pair, and when Mattie Owl left, Mrs. Cruikshank must have promptly sat down and copied the pattern in new yarn, because her family has knit mittens

---

*Instructions for the Fox and Geese pattern can be found in *Fox & Geese & Fences* (see bibliography).

Compass Mittens or Shooting Gloves

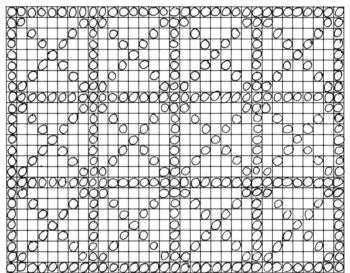

Materials: Briggs & Little's 2/12 knitting worsted, less than one skein each of lt and dk; or Bartlett-yarns 2-ply Fisherman Yarn, 2 to 3 ounces each of lt and dk. You can also use any worsted weight wool yarn.

Some of the names of this pattern—Compass and Spiderweb—suggest that the emphasis is meant to be on the long lines and their conjunctions, so although the pattern is very much like Fox and Geese, we chose colors that emphasized the lines and the centers much more than is usual in Fox and Geese, which is most often knitted in black or gray with a white background.

Equipment: 1 set Can. no. 13 (U.S. no. 1) dp knitting needles for ribbing. 1 set Can. no. 10 (U.S. no. 3) dp knitting needles, or size needed to knit the pattern to gauge. Yarn needle for finishing.

Gauge: 7 sts = 1 inch in Compass pattern.

Sizes: Child's 6 to 8 years (woman's small, woman's medium, man's medium, man's large).

Pattern: A multiple of 8 sts and 8 rounds. (Compass can only be knit flat if the second color is carried behind the work on the single-color row. If knitted flat, add a single lt st at the end to finish the pattern.)

The color of the lines and crosses (the contrast color) should be the one carried ahead.

Incs are made in the horizontal lines and in the triangles next to the vertical lines. For clarity's sake, one *band* means all eight rounds; one *block* means all eight sts in one round.

First round: K in contrast color (cc).

Second round: K 2 cc. Then, k 5 main color (mc), k 3 cc, around, ending with k 1 cc.

Third round: K 1 cc, k 1 mc, k 1 cc, k 3 mc, k 1 cc, k 1 mc around, ending with k 1 mc.

Fourth round: K 1 cc, k 2 mc, k 1 cc, k 1 mc, k 1 cc, k 2 cc, around, ending with k 2 mc.

Fifth round: K 1 cc, k 3 mc, and repeat around, ending with k 3 mc.

Sixth round: K 1 cc, k 2 mc, k 1 cc, k 1 mc, k 1 cc, k 2 mc, and end with k 2 mc. (This is the same as the fourth round.)

Seventh round: K 1 cc, k 1 mc, k 1 cc, k 3 mc, k 1 cc, k 1 mc. (This is the same as the third round.)

Eighth round: K 2 cc. Then, k 5 mc, k 3 cc around,

ending with k 1 cc. (Same as the second round.)

Since the second and eighth rounds contain 5 consecutive sts in one color, the yarn not in use should be caught up behind the work on both sides of the center st of each element.

Cuff: With main color (mc) and the smaller needles, cast on 39 (48, 54, 60, 66) sts, dividing them equally among three needles. K 2, p 1 in mc for 2½ (3, 3, 3, 3½) inches. Stripe with the contrasting color if you like; this helps when you plan to make two pairs of mittens from the same two skeins of yarn and want to consume equal amounts of both colors.

Change to larger needles by knitting one round in dk, at the same time increasing 9 (8, 6, 4, 6) sts, to a multiple of 8 sts, evenly spaced around. Total: 48 (56, 60, 64, 72) sts.

Begin pattern. For woman's small, start with the fifth round. All others start with the first round.

Woman's medium is not a multiple of 8 sts, but has 4 sts left over. Make these 4 sts a half-element of the pattern on the little-finger side of the palm, where it will be least noticeable. *Right hand:* K 3 blocks, k 1 half-block, k 4 blocks. *Left hand:* K 4 blocks, k 1 half-block, k 3 blocks.

Begin thumb gusset at the same time. For the right mitten the first block of pattern on the first needle forms the base of the thumb gusset; for the left mitten, it's the last block on the third needle.

Janetta retains the vertical lines at the beginning and end of this block and adds 2 sts within the lines every fourth round, keeping the center and verticals intact and increasing in the background color by knitting both colors into one of the cc sts. After the first band, she adds two more verticals and partial blocks on each side of the central thumb block as needed, so that the thumb gusset has one complete block running up the center, with an emerging half-block to each side.

Robin knits 2 blocks above the first thumb gusset block, adding 6 sts in the first pattern round (by looping as if to k and knitting both colors into 1 st), maintaining the pattern carefully. She starts the second round with two 6-st blocks, then incs 2 more sts in each block (by knitting both colors into 1 st) in the third pattern round.

Inc both sides of thumb gusset 4 (4, 4, 6, 6) times, for a total of 8 (8, 8, 12, 12) new sts, while knitting 1½ (2, 2, 3, 3) bands of pattern. Place the sts of the thumb gusset on a string, but leave the verticals on both sides on the needles.

Thumb gore increases.

Cast on 7 sts across the gap in pattern and continue to k in pattern.

For mittens: K 2½ (3, 3, 3½, 4) bands, then dec: At beginning of first needle, slip 1 st, k 1, and pass the slipped st over the knitted one; k to the third st from the center of the second needle and k 2

Chipman's Block Mittens in green and red, Fleur-de-lis and Diamonds Mittens in orange and white, brown Double-knit Cap with diamond pattern on crown.

(Top to bottom) Cunnin' Old-timey Baby Mittens, Tiny Labrador Diamonds Mitts, Double Irish Chain.

Double-knit cap with pattern on crown; Mrs. Martin's Finger Mitts in green; red and white Shining Star Mitts; Double-rolled Mittens in natural white; gray-and-white Shagged Loggers' Mittens; French-Canadian Toque with star pattern on brim.

Mittens with Shag on the Inside, Flying Geese Gloves.

(Top to bottom) Big Waves Mittens, Shepherd's Plaid Gloves, Labrador Snowflake Mittens, Shining Star Mitts.

Double-knit Cap and All-cuff Wristers in yellow, Double-rolled Mittens with red-and-green shagged cuffs, Partridge Feet Mittens.

Compass pattern in both mittens and shooting gloves.

(Left to right) Northern Star, Fleur-de-lis, and Partridge Feet mittens.

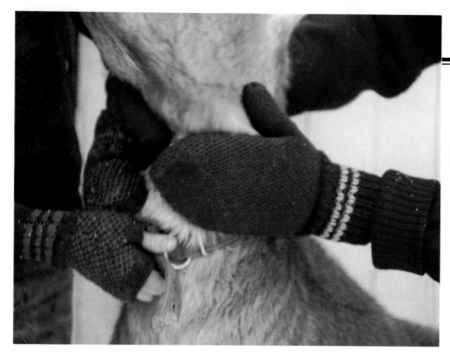

Salt and Pepper Wristers, Mittens
Hooked on a Dowel.

Baby's Patterned Cap and Mittens in
Chipman's Block, blue-and-white mittens
in Labrador Diamonds pattern.

together, k 1 (in most sizes a vertical line), slip 1, k 1 and pass the slipped st over the knitted st. Narrow in this way every other round 2 (2, 3, 4, 4) times, then put all the palm sts on one needle and all the back sts on another, divided equally, break the yarn, and with a yarn needle, graft across the end, stitching between back and palm sts in imitation of a row of stockinette st. Carry all ends to the wrong side of the fabric.

For hunter's mitts: After casting on sts across the thumb gap, k ¾ (1, 1, 1½, 1½) bands of pattern. Put unto a string the first 6 (7, 8, 9, 9) sts from the first needle and the last 6 (7, 8, 9, 9) sts from the third needle for the trigger finger. Cast on 4 (4, 6, 6, 6) sts over the gap and continue in pattern. If the pattern doesn't fit, sacrifice it between the fingers. K in pattern for 1½ (2, 2, 2½, 3) bands.

Dec: Begin to dec in the center of the second needle as for mittens (k 2 together, k 1, slip 1, pass the slipped st over the knitted st), decreasing every round only on the second needle, for 6 rounds. In the next round, dec once at the beginning of the first needle and the end of the third needle, and dec in the center of the second needle twice more. Arrange the remaining sts unto 2 needles, break yarn, and with a yarn needle graft across the end in the background color, stitching back and forth in imitation of a row of stockinette st.

Trigger finger: Pick up 6 sts at corners and edge of trigger-finger hole. Pick up sts from string and arrange all sts unto three needles. K in pattern for 2 (2½, 2½, 3, 3) bands.

Dec: K 1, k 2 together for 2 rounds. Pull both ends of yarn through remaining sts and pull up tightly, then take ends to inside of finger with a yarn needle. Darn them down.

Thumb: Pick up on one needle and k in pattern 9 sts at corners and back of thumb hole. Pick up on 2 needles and k in pattern 15 (15, 15, 19, 19) sts from string. If the number resulting is not evenly divisible by 8, the inside corner of the thumb next to the palm is the most inconspicuous place for a partial block. K in pattern for 1¾ (2, 2¼, 2½, 2¾) bands, or to tip of thumb. Dec for 2 rounds: k 1, k 2 together, maintaining pattern as well as you can, particularly the verticals. When 8 to 12 sts remain (depending on size), break yarn and pull up the remaining sts on both strands with a yarn needle. Carry both ends to the inside of the mitten and darn them into the inside surface.

(*Note:* Because the elements of this pattern are so large (8 by 8 sts), maintaining the pattern while executing a subtle variation in thumb size is almost impossible without using tricks. I add partial blocks; other knitters in Maine and Nova Scotia reknit a too-wide thumb with needles one size smaller.—J.D.)

Shooting gloves have a separate forefinger.

Chipman's Block Mittens

Chipman's block is a bit of feminine deception. At first glance it appears to be a check—little bands of dark and light interwoven diagonally—and maybe tricky to knit.

Look more closely: It's two rows of three light, three dark alternated with two rows of one light, one dark (otherwise known as Salt and Pepper). No little squares on the diagonal. In fact, no squares or diagonals at all.

Chipman's Block was sent to Janetta from New Brunswick, where Chipman has long been a common family name. The roots of this pattern seem to be British, and even today similar checks are knitted into mittens and gloves in England (McGregor, 1983) and Scotland, but to our knowledge, they lack the clever *trompe l'oeil* of this pattern.

This is a fun pattern to knit, mainly because it looks like something it isn't. It's quick and easy to work and is handsome in any size.

Chipman's Block Mittens

Materials: 2 to 3 ounces each lt and dk, fairly lightweight worsted wool yarn. The brown and white example in the color photo was knitted in Beehive Superwash Wool; the green and red example in Brunswick Yarns Germantown wool.

Equipment: 1 set Can. no. 13 (U.S. no. 1) dp knitting needles for the ribbing; 1 set Can. no. 11 (U.S. no. 3) dp knitting needles, or whatever size you need to knit the pattern to gauge.

Gauge: 7.5 sts = 1 inch in Chipman's Block pattern.

Sizes: Child's 2 to 4 (child's 4 to 6 years, child's 6 to 8, woman's small, woman's medium, man's medium, man's large).

Pattern: A multiple of 6 sts and 8 rounds, Chipman's Block can be knit flat if desired.

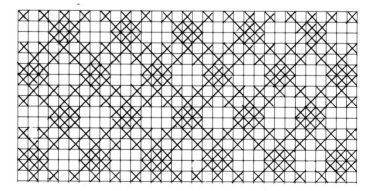

First round: K 1 dk, k 1 lt around.

Second round: K 3 lt, k 3 dk around.

Third round: Repeat second round.

70

Fourth round: K 1 dk, k 1 lt around.

Fifth round: K 1 lt, k 1 dk around.

Sixth round: K 3 dk, k 3 lt around.

Seventh round: Repeat sixth round.

Eighth round: K 1 lt, k 1 dk around.

Be sure to read General Instructions for Double-knitting before starting this project.

Cuff: With dk yarn and smaller needles, cast on 36 (42, 48, 51, 54, 60, 66) sts. K 2, p 1 for 1¾ (2, 2½, 2½, 3, 3, 3) inches of ribbed cuff.

Change to larger needles and k 1 round dk, increasing 2 (2, 2, 3, 2, 2, 2) sts per needle, for a total 42 (48, 54, 60, 60, 66, 72) sts.

Thumb gusset: The first 6 sts on the first needle for the right mitten and the last 6 sts of the third needle for the left mitten form the beginning of the thumb gusset. (It isn't really necessary to knit a left and a right mitten. Because of the way the tip of the hand is narrowed, this mitten can be used on either hand.)

Inc at the center of these 6 sts by knitting both colors into each of 2 adjacent sts of the Salt and Pepper. If you do this once in the first round of Salt and Pepper (1 lt, 1 dk) and twice in the next round, immediately above the first inc, you will have 6 new sts, or a whole pattern element, and the pattern will look right at first glance.

Inc this way 1 (1, 2, 2, 2, 3, 3) times. Continue knitting in pattern until 1½ (1¾, 2, 2½, 2¾, 2¾, 3) inches above the cuff.

Take off thumb gusset: Put on a string the 11 (11, 17, 17, 17, 23, 23) sts of the thumb gusset, cast on 5 sts over the gap, and k straight up in pattern 1½ (2, 2½, 3, 4, 4, 5) 8-round bands.

Dec by knitting 2 together in 12 adjacent sts in the Salt and Pepper rounds, maintaining the 1-1 alternation of colors. Do this on both sides now for child's size 2 to 4 and 4 to 6, but only on the little-finger side for the other sizes. K up in pattern to the next 2 rounds of Salt and Pepper and dec again: K 2 together 6 times on both forefinger and little-finger sides in all sizes. K to the next 2 rounds of Salt and Pepper and repeat this dec.

The smallest 2 sizes can be closed off here. Skip the next paragraph.

For the larger sizes, dec 6 sts each side every band of Salt and Pepper until about 42 sts remain. K 1, 2 together around for 2 rounds (in the next Salt and Pepper rounds), k 1 more round Salt and Pepper.

Break yarn, and pull up the remaining sts on the dk tail. Darn the dk tail back and forth, invisibly, over the tip.

Thumb: Pick up and k in pattern 7 sts from the back and corners of the thumb hole. Pick up and k in pattern the 11 (11, 17, 17, 17, 23, 23) sts from the string. K straight up in pattern for 1½ (1¾, 2, 2¼, 2½, 2¾, 3) inches.

Dec, on Salt and Pepper rounds: K 1, k 2 together, around, for 2 rounds. If more than 12 remain, k 2 rounds of 3 lt 3 dk without decreasing. Then dec: k 2 together around in Salt and Pepper.

Break yarn, draw the dk end firmly through the remaining sts, then darn back and forth across the tip.

Draw all ends to the inside of the mitten, turn it inside out, and darn all the tails into the inside surface. Turn it right side out and it's ready to wear.

Double-knits with a French Accent

Franco-American and Franco-Canadian women seem to be avid knitters from a way back, and while they knit some of the same patterns as their Anglo compatriots, they have others that are distinctly their own. Fleur-de-lis is one, but there are others.

In southwestern Nova Scotia, Acadian women do more mosaic knitting than double-knitting, knitting two colors but only one color per round, slipping all the stitches that will be in the other color (J.D.). This gives a curious raised texture to the fabric, while the back appears to be single-knit.

The New World French women in Maine and New Brunswick double-knit mittens and caps, though, as do the Acadian women of Cape Breton, whence our Fleur-de-lis mittens. There, too, Margaret Richard knits dandy boot socks with a simple double-knit pattern (which you won't find here—this is a mitten book, after all). But we have included a toque, the knitted wool cap with a turned-up, double-knit cuff.

Janetta has provided much information for this section, and the directions for Fleur-de-lis and Diamonds, which first appeared in her booklet, *Traditional Nova-Scotia Double-Knitting Patterns.*

—R.H.

Fleur-de-lis Mittens

Fleur-de-lis can be nothing but a French design. Even the name evokes images of the Sun King and the prerevolutionary French flag. In fact, Fleur-de-lis is widely knit by women of French descent in both New England and Canada for just this reason. The examples were knit in Charlos Cove, Nova Scotia, by Annie Pettipas, in the bright colors people like there.

However, the fleur-de-lis shape has other possibilities, the Boy Scouts being only one. Janetta Dexter reports that a non-French woman in Tatamagouche, Nova Scotia, knits the design into socks with the "lilies" in dark gray on a natural sheep's white background arranged not in diamonds but in vertical and horizontal lines. She calls this "Snowbirds," a local name for the snow buntings that come to the area when the winter is too severe in the Arctic. Snow buntings have white tummies and sparrowlike markings on their backs, so that they appear white when flying overhead, but gray against the snow.

In Iceland and the Faeroe Islands, the pattern is routinely knit into sweaters for the commercial market and apparently has no name there. It's also knit into the palms of Norwegian mittens more often than any other pattern.

This is a good project for a first bicolored mitten, as it has no thumb gore to fiddle with. It also has a simple pattern, and a plain-knit thumb. Although the multicolored example seems to have three colors in some rounds—a no-no in the rule books—this is an illusion. There are, in fact, only two.

This is one of several mittens in this collection that have no thumb gore. Joan Waldron of the Nova Scotia Museum in Halifax observed that women of English background seem to like the shape of

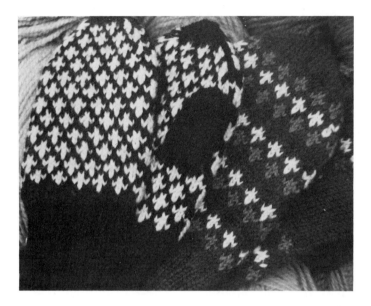

mittens with thumb gores, while women of French descent seem to prefer them without. I don't know whether this reflects the shape of their respective hands, but it is interesting that the mittens without thumb gores have additional stitches in their width to accommodate the thumb, although they tend to bind a little at the point where my (Anglo-German) thumb separates from my hand. Not all the goreless mittens here are from women of French ancestry or association; several of the Labrador mitts are knit without thumb gores, and one comes from Inuit women, whose knitting expertise originated with Norwegian Moravian missionaries.

—R.H.

Fleur-de-lis Mittens

Materials: Depending on size, 2 to 3 ounces dk and 2 to 3 ounces lt worsted weight yarn or 1 ounce each of three colors that complement the main color.

Equipment: 1 set Can. no. 10 (U.S. no. 3) dp knitting needles, or size you need to knit the pattern to the correct gauge. 1 set Can. no. 12 (U.S. no. 2) dp knitting needles for cuff. Yarn needle for finishing.

Gauge: 7 sts and 7 rounds = 1 square inch in Fleur-de-lis pattern.

Sizes: Child's 2 to 4 years (child's 4 to 6, child's 8 to 10, woman's small, woman's medium, man's medium, man's large).

Pattern: A multiple of 4 sts and 6 rounds. This pattern can be knit flat, but be sure to add a st to both ends for the seam.

Please read General Instructions for Double Knitting before starting this project.

And a final note: On the line where one round ends and the next begins, Annie Pettipas leaves off the final contrasting st that forms the petal of the lily in the new round. This looks better because the break in the pattern between rounds jams the 2 lilies into each other unattractively. (If this piece of information troubles you, ignore it. It's not essential.)

First round: k 1 contrast color (cc), k 3 main color (mc), around.

Second round: K 2 cc. Then, k 1 mc, k 3 cc around, ending with k 2 mc (skipping the last contrasting st).

Third round: Same as first round: k 1 cc, k 3 mc, around.

Fourth round: (New band of lilies. Change cc if you wish.) K 2 mc. Then, k 1 cc, k 3 mc around. End with k 1 mc.

Fifth round: K 1 mc. Then k 3 cc, k 1 mc around. End with k 3 cc.

Sixth round: Same as fourth round: K 2 mc. Then, k 1 cc, k 3 mc around. End with k 1 mc.

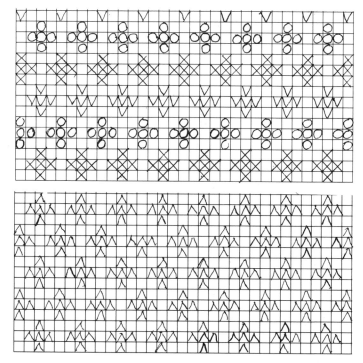

Fleur-de-lis: (top) in four colors, (bottom) in two colors.

Cuff: On smaller dp needles, cast on 39 (42, 45, 48, 51, 57, 63) sts. K 2, p 1 for 2 (2½, 2½, 3, 3, 3, 3½) inches.

Change to larger needles and k 1 round in background color, adding 8 (9, 7, 8, 9, 7, 9) sts evenly spaced for a total 44 (48, 52, 56, 60, 64, 72) sts.

These are the sts that make up for there being no thumb gore.

Start pattern in next round. K straight up in pattern for about 1¼ (1½, 2, 2¼, 2½, 2½, 3) inches to the thumb hole. Put the thumb hole between two pattern bands; don't split one in the middle.

The thumb hole will be placed at the beginning of the first needle for the right mitten and the end of the third needle for the left mitten. K a 12-inch length of a completely different color yarn into the first (or last) 6 (7, 8, 8, 9, 9, 11) sts. Then backtrack and reknit the same sts in pattern. (Later you will pick out this short piece of yarn, pick up the stitches that it used to connect, plus 2 on the sides, and have enough to knit the thumb.)

Hand: Continue knitting straight up in pattern for 1 (1¾, 2½, 2¾, 3, 3¼, 3¾) inches.

Dec: K to within 2 sts of the middle of the second needle; k 2 together, slip 1, k 1, pass the slipped st over the k st. This is the little-finger side. Repeat this dec every third round 0 (0, 1, 1, 1, 2, 2) times, only on the little-finger side. Maintain the pattern as well as you can.

Then dec both sides: On the first needle, slip 1, k 1, pass the slipped st over the k st. K to 2 sts before the middle st of the second needle. K 2 together, slip 1, k 1, pass the slipped st over the k st. K up to 2 sts before the end of the third needle. K 2 together.

Work this dec every second round 1 (1, 2, 2, 2, 3, 3) times, then every round.

When the decs start to come in every round, end the pattern with a completed band and continue decreasing in mc until about 6 sts remain.

Break yarn and graft the remaining sts together, or draw them up firmly on the tail. If you use the latter technique, darn the tail back and forth across the tip.

Thumb: Pick out the contrasting strand at the thumb hole and pick up 6 (7, 8, 8, 9, 9, 11) sts each from front and back of thumb hole and one from each corner, for a total 14 (16, 18, 18, 20, 20, 24) sts. Work the thumb in pattern if you wish, putting partial patterns on the palm side of the thumb, or k it plain, as is traditional.

(Note: In the example, the gauge of the thumb is 6.5 sts per inch in plain knit—slightly larger than the rest of the mitten. This is because of the difference in tension between plain, single-strand knitting and two-strand, patterned knitting. At this tension, 18 or 20 sts make a comfortable thumb for the large child's and woman's sizes, but will not if you continue to knit in pattern, with the 7-st-per-inch tension. You can either add 4 more sts to the original thumb hole by knitting the contrasting yarn in for 2 more sts, or k the thumb with the next size larger needles.)

K straight up 1¼ (1½, 2, 2, 2¼, 2¼, 2½) inches. Dec just as on the main part of the mitten until 6 sts remain. Break yarn, draw remaining sts up firmly on the tail. Darn the end invisibly back and forth across the tip.

Draw all tails into the mitten, turn it inside out, and darn them all down. Turn the mitten right side out and knit another!

Fleur-de-lis and Diamonds Mittens

Fleur-de-lis and Diamonds Mittens

Fleur-de-lis and Diamonds is a combination of two old patterns which is more effective than either alone. This combination is knit in Nova Scotia and New Brunswick, also on the island of Gotland, in Sweden, where it's called Goose-Eye (*The Swedish Mitten Book*, Lark, 1984). This doesn't necessarily mean it was brought to Nova Scotia by Swedish settlers. It may mean that it's a pattern with deep roots in a common past. Many of the patterns we consider traditionally part of New England or Atlantic Canada are also found in Scandinavia and the British Isles.

In both places, it's traditionally knit in a light yarn with a dark background.

Materials: Depending on size, 2 to 3 ounces dk and 2 to 3 ounces lt worsted weight wool yarn.

Equipment: 1 set U.S. no. 4 (Can. no. 9) dp knitting needles, or size needed to knit to gauge. 1 set U.S. no. 2 (Can. no. 11) dp knitting needles for ribbed cuff. Yarn needle for finishing.

Gauge: 7 sts = 1 inch in Fleur-de-lis and Diamonds pattern.

Sizes: Child's 2 to 4 years (child's 6 to 8, child's 8 to 10, woman's medium, man's medium, man's large).

Pattern: A multiple of 8 sts and 8 rounds. This pattern can be knit flat.

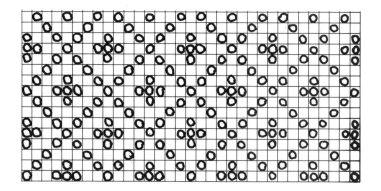

The graph shows the pattern and a possible adjustment for the inside of the thumb when the thumb stitches don't come out to an even multiple of 8. This occurs in child's size 2 to 4 and man's medium and large.

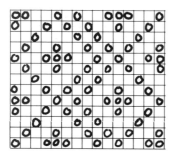

Thumb detail for child's size 2 to 4 and man's medium and large.

Knitters on the northeast coast of England are said to memorize the complicated stitch patterns for gansey sweaters by chanting them. You might try this technique with some of these patterns—especially the long ones. You'll find they have a rhythm to them once you start.

However, this pattern doesn't really need to be memorized. When you've done a few rounds, you'll be able to see what comes next with no trouble.

First round: K 1 lt, k 2 dk, k 3 lt, k 2 dk around, ending with k 2 dk.

Second round: K 1 dk, k 1 lt, k 2 dk, k 1 lt, k 2 dk, k 1 lt, around, ending with k 1 lt.

Third round: K 2 dk. Then, k 1 lt, k 3 dk around, ending with k 1 dk.

Fourth round: K 1 lt, k 2 dk, k 1 lt, k 1 dk, k 1 lt, k 2 dk, around, ending with k 2 dk.

Fifth round: K 2 lt. Then, k 2 dk, k 1 lt, k 2 dk, k 3 lt around, ending with k 1 lt.

Sixth round: K 1 lt, k 2 dk, k 1 lt, k 1 dk, k 1 lt,

k 2 dk around, ending with k 2 dk (same as fourth round).

Seventh round: K 2 dk. Then, k 1 lt, k 3 dk around, ending with k 1 dk (same as third round).

Eighth round: K 1 dk, k 1 lt, k 2 dk, k 1 lt, k 2 dk, k 1 lt, ending with k 1 lt.

Please read General Instructions for Double Knitting for pointers before starting this project.

Cuff: On smaller dp knitting needles and using dk yarn, cast on 39 (48, 51, 54, 60, 63) sts, arranged so that the first and third needles have an equal number of sts and the second needle, the odd number. (Life will also be easier if each needle starts with k 2 and ends with p 1. Then you can knit ribbing in the car at night or at the movies.)

K 2, p 1 straight up for 1½ (2, 2½, 3, 3, 3½) inches.

Change to larger dp knitting needles and k 1 round in dk, adding 1 (0, 5, 2, 4, 9) sts to make a multiple of 8 sts.

Start pattern in next round. Begin thumb gusset immediately: The first 8 sts on the first needle of the right mitten and the last 8 sts of the third needle of the left mitten form the base of the thumb gusset. You may think this will be easy to keep track of, but in this pattern it isn't, so please put a marker between the eighth and ninth sts from the end.

To keep the pattern straight on the thumb gusset, keep an eye firmly on the series of diamonds running up the middle, inc only at the edges of the thumb gusset, building new pattern elements out from the center one. Inc by knitting both colors into 1 st, or, if this isn't possible while maintaining the pattern, by picking up and knitting a st from the preceding round. Be sure the colors of your inc sts follow the pattern on the thumb gusset. *Don't* look at how it fits the pattern on the rest of the mitten or you may lose your nerve. It will look great when you're done.

Inc at both edges of thumb gusset 2 (2, 3, 3, 4, 5) times, every fourth round, for a total of 12 (12, 14, 14, 18, 18) sts on the thumb gusset. Continue knitting until 1¼ (1½, 2, 2½, 2½, 3) inches above the cuff.

Put all thumb gusset sts on a string and cast on 8 sts over the gap. Total: 40 (48, 56, 56, 64, 72) sts.

K straight up for 1¾ (2, 2½, 3½, 4, 4½) inches. This should be roughly to the tip of the little finger.

Dec: On the first needle, slip 1, k 1, pass the slipped st over the st. K (in pattern) to 2 sts from the middle of second needle and k 2 sts together, slip 1, k 1, pass the slipped st over the k st. K to 2 sts from the end of the third needle, k 2 together.

Generally, it looks best if the sts in a progression of slipped-st decs alternate in color or are mostly in the background color. You can control this: the st that will show here is the first k st after the slipped st.

Dec every second round 1 (2, 2, 3, 4, 4) times. Then dec every round util 14 (16, 16, 16, 20, 24) sts remain.

Divide these equally on 2 needles, all palm sts on 1 needle, all back sts on the other. With a yarn needle, graft across the end, using the background color, and stitching back and forth in imitation of a row of stockinette st.

Thumb: Pick up on 2 needles the 12 (12, 14, 14, 18, 18) sts from the thumb gusset. With the third needle, pick up and k 6 (8, 10, 10, 10, 10) sts from the back and corners of the thumb hole. Total: 18 (20, 24, 24, 28, 28) sts.

For child's sizes 2 to 4 and man's sizes medium and large, the pattern will not quite fit the thumb. Use the pattern from the second graph on the inner, hidden side of the thumb, fitting it carefully into the rest of the pattern on the thumb.

K straight up in pattern 1½ (2, 2¼, 2½, 2½, 3) inches. Then dec sharply: k 1, k 2 together until about 6 to 10 sts remain.

Break yarn and draw one strand through the remaining sts. Pull up firmly. Draw the other strand inside the mitten. Darn the first strand invisibly back and forth across the tip to make a smooth, rounded finish.

Turn the mitten inside out and darn down all tails. Turn it right side out, and it's ready to wear.

—J.D.

Diamonds and Waves
from Newfoundland and Labrador

In Newfoundland and Labrador, the style of mittens changes radically from the all-over patterns knit in Maine, New Brunswick, and Nova Scotia. A blending of traditions—Norwegian, Channel Islands, Irish and Scottish—results in something different and special.

Knitting in two colors is not called double-knitting here, but two-ball knitting, or double-ball knitting. The pattern doesn't wrap around the mitten, but is confined to the back, with the rest usually knit in Salt and Pepper. In Newfoundland, mittens are called "cuffs" or sometimes "thumbies" (Pocius, 1979) and knitting needles are called "skivvies."

Sometimes the pattern is markedly Scandinavian, like the Shining Star and Snowflake patterns shown in the following pages. It may be one of the many patterns of checks or diamonds that knitters seem fond of here, or waves, running either lengthwise or across the hand. Sometimes it is a combination: a snowflake pattern surrounded by diamonds, a checked pattern with Fleur-de-lis on the palm.

More often than anywhere else in Maine and Maritime Canada, the index finger will be separated, or the handcovering will be a complete glove with all the fingers separated. Sometimes the ends of the mitten will be rounded, as they are farther south; other mitts, usually those with a strongly Norwegian look, will also have the pointed Norwegian hand and thumb tips.

Knitting mitts and socks and handspinning the wool of one's own sheep are still viable home crafts in both Newfoundland and Labrador, and many families maintain traditional patterns. Knitters also play with patterns, changing a stitch here or there, taking a little of the drudgery out of excessive knitting. Every pair of Diamond mitts seems to be different.

Although Newfoundland folklorist Jerry Pocius wrote that knitting in Newfoundland is now mainly recreational—a hobby—the fact that almost everyone owns a pair of two-ball mittens or gloves shows the importance of handknitting here in comparison with further south, where whole communities have forgotten the skill of double-knitting wool mittens or turning the heel of a sock.

Mrs. Martin's Finger Mitts

Them Days: Stories of Early Labrador is a quarterly devoted to interviews with local people about "them days" past, much like *Salt* and *Foxfire* in the United States. In 1981, *Them Days* researcher Doris Saunders recorded Harriet Pardy Martin telling how to knit a finger mitt (or hunter's mitt), one with the index finger separate.

Mrs. Martin's account is so to the point and so complete that we are reproducing it here as the basic set of instructions for the Labrador Diamonds and Waves patterns. Most of the mitts and finger mitts in this section are knit using her instructions, which make knitting the palm and back in different patterns easier.

Mrs. Martin's diamonds are the first graph. Variations on the Diamonds and one Wave design are shown beneath. All have a multiple of seven stitches and can be substituted for each other, for the checks on the Labrador gloves, and for the diamonds on the Tiny Diamond Mittens for babies. One can arrange all of the diamond patterns either in checkerboard arrangements, or as Mrs. Martin

has done, in broad vertical stripes. Each pattern and each arrangement has its own dynamic and speaks highly of the design sense of these knitters of the subarctic.

Here, now, Mrs. Martin:

> I learned to knit when I was a very small girl. I used to make doll's clothes. Sometimes 'twould come out good, other times 'twould be really funny. I knits like Aunt Mary Lemare, holds my needles like she used to.

> Aunt Mary was the one who taught me how to knit mitts. I was sixteen then. Mary is a few years younger than me.

> The first pair of finger mitts that I made was a woman's pair. I makes them for men, women, children, and babies now. I mostly used the diamond pattern when I started makin' mitts at first. After I got married, Ethel Coombs showed me how to do the deer and snowflake pattern. I likes white and black best, and I likes three-ply wool, kind of soft.

> When I'm makin' finger mitts for a woman, I take four size 10 needles and cast on 40 sts, 12 on 1 needle, 16 on the other and 12 on the third needle. On the band I k 10 rows of main color [mc], 3 rows of contrast color [cc], 1 mc, 3 cc, and 9 mc. Now rearrange the sts so's there will be 10 on 1 needle, 20 on the second needle and 10 on the third. The 20 will be the back of the mitt. I add sts now according to the size I want, for this pair, I'll add 4, 8, 4.

> On the first needle I'll k 6, add 1, k 1, add 1, k 1, add 1, k 1, add 1, k 1; that's 14 sts. Now on the back I'll k 6, add and k the same as on the first needle to the last 6 sts, k them. The last needle

is done opposite to the first one. Now I have 14, 28, and 14 sts.

Now for the pattern, on the front needles you k 1 mc, 1 cc, 1 mc and so on, and change each row to get the checkered pattern [Salt and Pepper]. Now for the back, you start off, 3 mc, 1 cc, 3 mc, 3 cc, 1 mc, 3 cc, 3 mc, 1 cc, 3 mc, 3 cc, 1 mc, 3 cc. When I starts up for the thumb [immediately], I k 1 cc, 5 sts [mc, cc, mc, cc, mc], and 2 cc. Each following row I adds 2 more sts 'till I gets to 14 sts between the 2 solid lines of cc. Some people don't

add sts for the thumb part. I likes the shape you gets when you adds on. When you gets up to where you want your thumb, leave 14 sts on a st holder. [Cast on 5 sts over the gap.]

Now you continue knitting on the main part of the mitt to where you wants the finger [at the top of 4 diamonds]. Take 7 sts from the first needle, and pick up 7 [2 from the first needle, cast on 3 over the gap and 2 from the third needle] on the second, and take 7 from the last needle. K up 21 rows.

To cast off, k 3 sts together. This keeps the checkered pattern even. Cast off until there is only 1 st left on each of the 3 needles. Break both pieces of wool and thread it [either, or both] on a darning needle and finish off the finger.

The main part of the mitt is 10, 21, and 10. K up 22 rows and cast off as you did the finger. The thumb is 7, 7, 7, and 18 rows. Cast off again as with the finger.

Do the same things for the other mitt, rememberin' to put the thumb on the opposite side. You wouldn't want 2 mitts for one hand.

There is one thing to remember: you hold the main color ahead of the contrast color. If you hold the contrast color ahead of the main color, you'll get a ridge in your knitting. The main color has to be ahead *all* the time.*

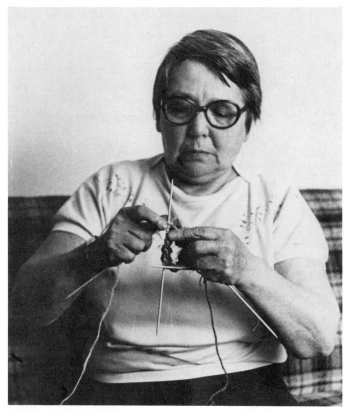

Harriet Pardy Martin.

*In my experience, it doesn't matter too much which color you carry ahead in this pattern as long as you're consistent. Both colors are emphasized equally in this case. —R.H.

Mrs. Martin's Finger Mitts— With More Sizes

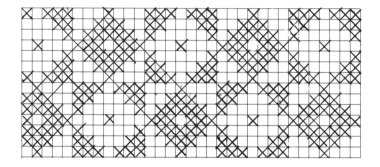

Materials: 2 to 3 ounces each lt and dk worsted weight wool yarn. We've used Bartlettyarns 2-ply Fisherman Yarn (blue and white Diamond mitt in color photo), Charity Hill Farm worsted (Hardwick, MA 01037) (green finger mitts), but Briggs & Little 2/12 or 2/8 will work equally well and is probably what Mrs. Martin uses. The 2/8 makes a much heavier mitten with the same gauge.

Equipment: 1 set Can. no. 9 (U.S. no. 4) dp knitting needles are used throughout, or the size you need to knit to gauge.

Sizes: Child's 4 to 6 years (child's 8 to 10, woman's medium, man's medium, man's large).

Gauge: 6.5 sts = 1 inch in Salt and Pepper pattern.

Patterns: All of these patterns have two 7-st elements. If the number of sts on the back of the hand is a multiple of 7, just start at a bottom corner of the chart and knit.

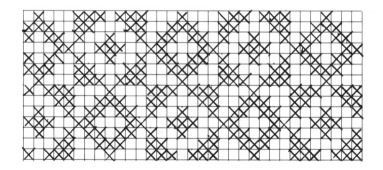

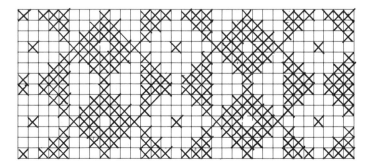

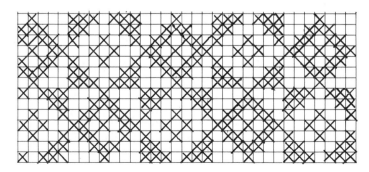

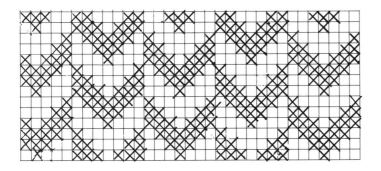

If the number of sts on the back of the hand doesn't quite work, try to have either the vertical line between two adjoining pattern elements or the center st of an element in the middle of the back, and take off as many sts as necessary from both sides equally, so that the pattern looks balanced. If you need to add a st in the middle of the back of the hand to have the center st really in the center, do so.

Note: The first round and the seventh round of the Diamond patterns are identical and both are used, usually.

Please read General Instructions for Double-Knitting before starting this project.

Cuff: Cast on 32 (36, 40, 44, 48) sts with main color (mc). K 3, p 1 for 10 rounds in mc, then 3 rounds in contrast color (cc), 1 round of mc, 3 more rounds of cc, and 9 rounds of mc. (Knitters in this part of Canada are partial to having 26 rounds in their mitten cuffs; although the stripes may vary in number and width, the cuffs all seem to have 26 rounds.)

Now arrange the sts so that one-quarter are on the first needle, one-half are on the second needle, and the last quarter are on the third needle.

Inc by knitting into the loop between sts:

For child's 4 to 6, inc 3 on the first needle, 6 on the second, 3 on the third, for a total 11, 22, and 11.

For a child's 8 to 10, inc 3 on the first needle, 6 on the second, and 3 on the third. Totals: 12, 24, 12.

For woman's medium, inc 4 on the first needle, 8 on the second, and 4 on the third. Totals: 14, 28, 14.

For man's medium, inc 5 on the first needle, 10 on the second, 5 on the third. Totals: 16, 32, 16.

For man's large, inc 6 on the first needle, 12 on the second, 6 on the third. Totals: 18, 36, 18.

Start pattern: K Salt and Pepper on the first and third needles, and follow the Diamond or Wave pattern of your choice on the second needle.

Start the thumb gore in the same round: For the right mitten, on the first needle, k 1 mc, k 1 cc, up to 8 sts before the end of needle, then k 2 cc. K 1 mc, k 1 cc for 5 sts, then k 1 cc. The 2 cc and the final cc sts mark the outer edges of the thumb gore. Inc by knitting both colors into the first and last Salt and Pepper sts within these 2 marking lines, every round until you have 13 (13, 15, 19, 21) sts. Be careful to keep the colors in the right order when you inc.

For the left mitten, reverse this. Put the single cc st on the first st and the 2 cc marker on the seventh and eighth sts of the third needle.

K straight up in pattern until 1¼ (1¾, 2, 2, 2½) inches above cuff. Put all the thumb gore sts between, but not including, the 2 cc lines on a string, cast on 5 sts over the gap and continue straight up in pattern for 1¼ (1¾, 2, 2, 2½) inches above the thumb hole (the same distance as from the cuff to the thumb hole). If you have the hand you're knitting for available, simply measure the distance from the base of the fingers to the lower edge of the palm. Divide by 2 and see if that's about where the thumb separates from the hand. Adjust accordingly if it isn't.

Trigger Finger: If you have enough needles in the right size, you can k the trigger finger without putting anything on a string. Otherwise, put the trigger finger sts on a string and k the main part of the hand first.

For the trigger finger, take 5 (6, 7, 8, 9) sts from the first needle and the same number from the third needle onto 2 new needles. Pick up 2 more sts from the first needle on a new second needle, cast on 1 (2, 3, 4, 4) sts over the gap, and pick up 2 more from the third needle. Total: 15 (18, 21, 24, 26) sts. If you have an even number, add or subtract 1 st (depending on which gives the better fit) to make the pattern work.

K straight up in Salt and Pepper (all the way around) until 3¾ (4¼, 4½, 4½, 5) inches above the thumb hole, or until halfway up the fingernail of the index finger.

Dec sharply: K 2 together at both ends of all 3 needles, maintaining pattern, until 6 to 8 sts remain. Break yarn, draw the dk yarn firmly through the remaining sts and darn it neatly across the fingertip. (Notice I did not suggest knitting 3 sts together, as Mrs. Martin did, as I feel it tends to weaken the knit.)

Hand: K straight up in Salt and Pepper until 3½ (3¾, 4, 4, 4½) inches above the thumb hole, or to the base of the nail of the ring finger.

Dec: K 2 together, starting with a dk st, at both ends of every needle, every round, maintaining

pattern perfectly, until only 8 to 12 (depending on size) remain.

Break yarn, draw the remaining sts up on the dk strand, and darn it invisibly back and forth over the tip.

Thumb: Pick up from the string 12 (14, 16, 18, 20) sts on 2 needles. Pick up and k, in Salt in Pepper, 7 sts from the back and corners of the thumb hole. K straight up in Salt and Pepper for 1¾ (2, 2¼, 2½, 3) inches.

Dec: K 2 together at both ends of each needle, every round, until 6 to 8 sts remain. Break yarn, draw the dark strand through the remaining sts, and darn it back and forth over the tip.

Draw all tails to the inside of the mitt, turn it inside out, and darn in all ends.

Shepherd's Plaid Gloves

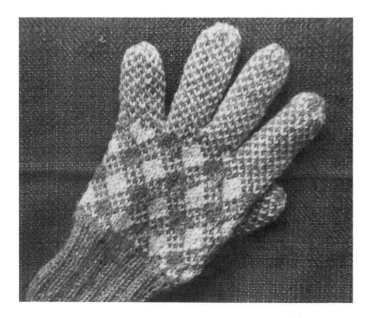

These very simple work gloves are probably the most universal double-knit handcovering in Newfoundland and Labrador. The checked pattern probably formed the beginning of the Diamonds pattern, as this pattern is often knit with one more row in the middle of the solid diamonds and a single contrasting stitch in the center. They seem also to be the basis of the mittens and finger mitts, because the checked or diamond pattern is usually only carried to the base of the fingers on mittens, much as if they were meant to be gloves but the knitter got tired of knitting.

The pair that formed the model for these was lent to me in Halifax, Nova Scotia, by Elizabeth Eve, who had bought them in Newfoundland.

I have seen photocopies of identical Scottish gloves from the Museum of Agricultural History and Rural Life, in England, complete with the prick in the center of each solid square, so there's not much question about their roots.

Like several of the French patterns and other Labrador patterns in this book, these gloves have no thumb gore. This makes them easier to knit, of course, and they do have room for the thumb. Knitters who make mittens without thumb gores add just about as many stitches as do thumb gore knitters. The difference is that they're added all at once, all around the base of the hand, rather than in a gradual triangle; and they're usually not taken off after the thumb hole. This makes a looser, less tailored-looking glove.

Although the originals are work gloves, I've added some refinements by making the little finger come off sooner than the others, and by making it shorter than the other fingers, so that, knitted in a soft worsted weight yarn, it need not be relegated to gardening and housepainting.

—R.H.

Shepherd's Plaid Gloves

Materials: 2 to 3 ounces each dk and lt worsted weight yarn, depending on size. Traditionally, these are knit in gray and cream-colored natural wool, often homespun.

Equipment: 1 set Can. no. 8 (U.S. no. 5) dp knitting needles, or size you need to knit the pattern to gauge.

Gauge: 6 st = 1 inch in Salt and Pepper pattern.

Sizes: Child's 4 to 6 years (child's 8 to 10 years, woman's medium, man's medium, man's large).

Patterns: Salt and Pepper and Checks.

A multiple of 2 sts and 2 rounds, Salt and Pepper alternates rounds of k 1 dk, k 1 lt with rounds of k 1 lt, k 1 dk. When it's worked in the round on an uneven number of sts, as it is on the fingers of this glove, the alternation occurs automatically.

The Checks pattern is a multiple of 10 sts and 12 rounds. With its two rounds of Salt and Pepper and its two rounds of 5 dk, 5 lt alternation, Checks is closely related to Chipman's Block.

If there is a multiple of 5 sts on the second needle in the size you're knitting, just follow the graph. If not, try to center the graphed pattern on the glove by locating the center st of a diamond in the center of the back; take sts off from both sides equally, marking the graph with a pencil so you'll know where you are for the first few rounds. Please note: The pattern has 2 rounds of 5 dk, 5 lt in the center of each check. This emphasizes the widest

point of the diamonds better than a single row of k 5 lt, k 5 dk.

Please read General Instructions for Double Knitting before starting this project.

Cuff: Cast on 30 (36, 42, 48, 54) sts on three needles, using main color (mc). K 2, p 1 for 2 (2½, 3, 3, 3½) inches, striping if you wish.

K 1 round in mc, adding 1 st between the 2 k sts of each rib, for a total of 40 (48, 56, 64, 72) sts. Rearrange sts so that one half are on the second needle and one quarter are on each of the other 2 needles. The first st of the round should still start the first needle. This will be the center of the palm; the second needle is the back of the hand.

For the right glove the thumb will come at the beginning of the third needle. For the left glove, the thumb will be at the end of the first needle. Add 4 more sts in this area in the first round of pattern by knitting both colors into 1 st. There are no more increases.

Start patterns: K Checks pattern on second needle and Salt and Pepper on first and third needles. If the pattern doesn't work at the joint between the first and third needles, add 1 st by knitting both colors into 1 st, in the correct order. K in pattern for 9 (11, 13, 15, 17) rounds.

Take off for the thumb. For the right glove, k to the third needle in pattern, k first st, then k 8 (10, 10, 12, 12) sts with a different piece of yarn in a brightly contrasting color. Backtrack and k the marking sts again, this time in pattern. (You will pick out the contrasting yarn later, pick up the sts it used to join plus 2 from the corners, and have enough sts for the thumb.)

For the left glove, use the last (but one) 8 (10, 10, 12, 12) sts on first needle.

86

K straight up in pattern for 6 (8, 10, 12, 14) more rounds, then take off for little finger: Put on a string 4 (6, 6, 7, 9) sts from the end of the second needle and 5 (7, 7, 9, 10) sts from the beginning of the third needle. Cast on 2 sts over the gap and k 3 more rounds.

Ring finger: Put on a separate needle 6 (7, 8, 9, 10) sts from the second needle, and on another needle 6 (7, 8, 9, 10) sts from the beginning of the third needle. Cast on 1 st over the gap, arrange the 13 (15, 17, 19, 21) sts on 3 needles and k up straight 1¾ (2¼, 2¾, 2¾, 3¼) inches in Salt and Pepper, or up to the fingertip.

Ring finger dec: K 2 together at both ends of all 3 needles, maintaining pattern, every round until 6 remain. Break yarn, pull up the remaining sts on the dark strand and tuck this finger into the glove, so it's out of your way.

Middle finger: Pick up and k 6 (7, 8, 8, 9) sts from the second needle, 2 (3, 1, 2, 2) sts from the base of the ring finger, and 6 (6, 8, 8, 9) from the third needle. Cast on 1 (1, 2, 1, 1) st over the gap and k straight up in Salt and Pepper for 2 (2½, 3, 3, 3½) inches, or to the fingertip. Dec and close off as for the ring finger, and tuck this finger into the glove.

Forefinger: Arrange the remaining 13 (14, 17, 19, 21) sts on 2 needles, pick up and k 2 (3, 2, 2, 2) sts from the base of the middle finger. K straight up in Salt and Pepper for 1¾ (2½, 2¾, 2¾, 3¼) inches, or to the fingertip. Close off.

Little finger: Pick up 2 sts from the base of the ring finger, take the sts off the string onto 3 needles, and k straight up in Salt and Pepper for 1½ (2, 2½, 2½, 3) inches. Close off.

Thumb: Pick out the strand of contrasting yarn that marks the thumb hole. Pick up from the bottom of the hole 8 (10, 10, 12, 12) sts. Pick up and k in pattern 2 sts from the palm-side corner and the 7 (9, 9, 11, 11) little loops at the top of the hole. Pick up and k 1 st from the outside corner. K straight up in pattern 1½ (2, 2¼, 2½, 3) inches. Close off as for the fingers.

If possible, try the glove on at this point. Nothing is irreversible until you finish off the ends.

Finish: Draw all ends, except those used to draw up the finger ends, into the glove. Run a skinny broomstick or other rounded stick up into the thumb, and darn across the end with the finishing strand neatly and invisibly. Do this with all the fingers. Draw these ends into the glove too.

Darn in all ends. Now is the time to give an extra tug to the tails that begin the fingers and the thumbs so that these sts are not big and ugly, and to prevent holes here. Darn these ends in, too. Knit one more.

Labrador Diamonds Mittens or Shooting Gloves

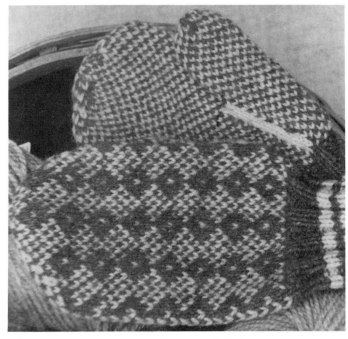

This pattern was taken from a child's mitt knitted in the Saint Anthony's area of Newfoundland, not Labrador. But all the families I met in the Happy Valley area of Labrador had similar mitts, so the name is not too far off base.

Usually the design is knitted only to the base of the fingers and Salt and Pepper is used from there to the tip of the mitten. I've carried the design all the way up the fingers because it looks smashing that way. I hope that's an adequate excuse for changing someone's traditional design slightly.

Decreases are on both edges of the back every round, and scattered, one to a round, on the palm, which is knitted in Salt and Pepper. Although I have heard that women in the area decrease by

This pattern was first published in *Needlecraft for Today,* 1985.

knitting three stitches together in Salt and Pepper, knitting two together twice side by side gives the same effect and doesn't weaken the knit as much.

—R.H.

Labrador Diamonds Mittens or Shooting Gloves

Materials: Labrador Diamonds is traditionally knit in a dark color with white or natural sheep's cream as a contrasting color. Depending on the size, you'll need 2 to 3 ounces dk and 2 to 3 ounces lt worsted weight wool yarn (or medium weight wool yarns from Briggs & Little).

Equipment: 1 set U.S. no. 4 (Can. no. 9) dp knitting needles, or size needed to k the gauge. 1 set U.S. no. 2 (Can. no. 13) dp knitting needles for the ribbed cuff. Yarn needle for finishing.

Gauge: 7 sts = 1 inch in Salt and Pepper pattern.

Sizes: Child's 4 to 6 (child's 8 to 10, woman's small, woman's medium, man's medium, man's large). Child's 4 to 6 is in mittens only, no shooting gloves.

Patterns: Diamonds, a variant of the checked patterns rampant in Newfoundland, is 8 sts wide and 6 rounds high. It is worked only on the back of these mittens. (One can use any of the Newfoundland/Labrador diamond patterns on the back of this mitten. See Mrs. Martin's Finger Mitts and Tiny Labrador Diamonds Mitts.)

Salt and Pepper, the most common pattern throughout the area, is also the simplest, a 2-st alternation of 2 colors, k 1 dk, k 1 lt. This is reversed every other round to give a speckled appearance.

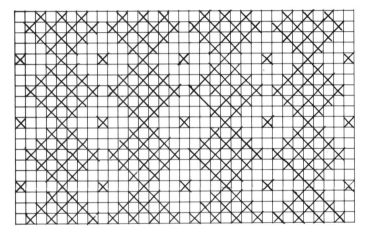

Please read General Instructions for Double-knitting before starting this project.

Cuff: Using dk yarn and the smaller needles, cast on 44 (48, 52, 56, 60, 64) sts. K 3, p 1 in dk for 10 rounds, lt for 3 rounds, dk for 2 rounds, lt for 3 rounds, and dk for 8 more rounds.

Change to larger needles and k 1 round dk. Rearrange the sts so that half (less 1) are on the second needle and the rest are divided equally between the first and third needles. The needle with half the sts will be the back of the mitten. The end of the round will be in the middle of the palm.

Start pattern and thumb gore in the next round.

Left mitten, palm: K 1 dk, k 1 lt until 6 sts from end of needle, then form the base of the thumb gore: k 2 lt, k both colors into the next st, dk then lt,

then k 1 dk, k both colors into the next st, lt then dk, k 1 lt. The 3 lt sts on the ends of this increase mark the outside edges of the thumb gore. Maintain these marking lines in each round.

Back: K Diamonds pattern on the second needle. If the number of sts on the back is a multiple of 8, begin at the lower right corner of the graph and work across. If not, adjust the pattern so that a vertical progression of either dark or speckled diamonds is centered on the center st of the back. Then take off sts equally from both sides. For example, if you have 29 sts on the back, the center st would be the fifteenth. Divide 8 into 29 to get 3 whole patterns and 5 leftover sts. The center of the second pattern should then be on the fifteenth st, and the 5 sts should be divided between the two edges.

Palm (on third needle): K 1 dk, k 1 lt to end of needle. The color of the next st should be the same color as your last st to make the checkered effect. If it isn't, undo the last st and k both colors into it, in the right order. You should only have to do this in 1 round.

Inc between the 2 white lines every 2nd round by knitting both colors into the marking st on the thumb gore side, or the st next to it, until there are 11 (12, 13, 14, 15, 16) thumb gore sts between the lt marking lines. Put these on a piece of string and cast on 6 (5, 6, 7, 8, 9) sts over the gap with the color in the correct order to carry on the palm pattern. Discontinue the 2 white verticals.

For mittens: Continue knitting in pattern straight up 2½ (3¼, 3½, 3¾, 4, 4¼) inches above the thumb hole.

Next round, k up to 2 sts from the little-finger edge of the back. K 2 sts together in the appropriate color. At beginning of the next needle, k 2 together in right color to fit into palm pattern. Dec 2 each round on the little-finger side 3 times, then dec 4 each round, 1 at each end of the back needle and 1 at each edge of the palm, carefully maintaining the pattern, until 12 sts remain. Break yarn and draw these 12 sts up on the dk tail. Darn the dk tail neatly into the tip.

For shooting gloves (no instructions for child's size 4 to 6): After taking off the thumb gore sts, continue knitting straight up in pattern (2, 2½, 2½, 2¾, 3) inches.

Then put on a string (6, 7, 7, 7, 8) sts from the thumb-side front, and (6, 6, 7, 7, 8) sts from the thumb-side back. Cast on (5, 6, 7, 7, 7) sts over the gap.

Continue the patterns and k up (20, 21, 22, 24, 25) rounds, then dec according to mitten instructions above.

Trigger finger: Put (12, 13, 14, 14, 16) sts from the string onto 2 needles. With the third needle, pick up (5, 6, 7, 7, 7) sts from the edge of the hole. Total: (17, 19, 21, 21, 23) sts. K 1 dk, k 1 lt for (18, 20, 21, 22, 24) rounds, then dec by knitting 2 together at both ends of needle, in pattern, until there are only 2 sts left on each needle. Draw these sts up on the dk strand, then darn back and forth over the tip in dk.

Thumb (all sizes, both styles): Pick up on 2 needles the 19 (19, 21, 23, 25, 27) sts from the thumb gore. On the third needle, pick up and k 8 (7, 8, 9, 10, 11) sts from the top and corners of the hole in correct color to continue the palm pattern uninterrupted. K up in Salt and Pepper pattern 14 (15, 17, 18, 19, 21) rounds.

Dec: k 2 together at both ends of each needle, in pattern, until 6 sts remain. Break yarn and draw these sts up on the dk strand. Darn the dk end into the tip.

Draw all other tails into the mitten and darn them into the inside surface of the fabric.

Big Waves for Big Mittens

Waves are a recurring theme in Newfoundland and Labrador mittens, and all the waves are pointed. One wave pattern—surely the easier to knit—is included in the graph as an alternative for Diamond mitts and gloves. A second one is presented here, with all the peculiarities of traditional knitting. This pattern, as is, makes only a man's large mitten, but it was so spectacular that I couldn't leave it out.

Phyllis Montague, of Northwest River, Labrador, had this mitten in a bag of patterns her mother (from St. Anthony's, Newfoundland) had made her that also included a Caribou mitt and the one I call Shining Star. This waves one was huge but grand! I photographed it and reconstructed the knitting by counting sts in the photograph. Mrs. Montague herself didn't knit many of these; she felt that mittens with deer (caribou) sold more readily.

This Wave pattern has many long leaps between color changes, which necessitates catching up the other color behind the work, a process that invariably causes some lumps. If you don't want to catch up the other color and can control your tension, you could make a pair, then wash them in cool water, scrubbing and rubbing them to encourage the loops to adhere to the inside surface. But you would have to exercise care in putting them on until they became somewhat matted together.

If you are inventive and like this pattern, maybe you can figure out how to make it smaller—either by using a finer yarn and needles, or by cutting down the design itself. A fingering yarn at nine stitches to the inch will bring it down to a woman's medium without altering the pattern.

—R.H.

Big Waves Mittens, on left.

Big Waves Mittens

Materials: About 3 ounces each lt and dk worsted weight yarn. I used Bartlettyarns 2-ply Fisherman Yarn, which is a little lighter than Briggs & Little 2/8, and a little heavier than Brunswick Yarns Germantown.

The example was knit in navy blue and natural cream-colored yarn, just like Mrs. Montague's.

Equipment: One set Can. no. 10 (U.S. no. 3) dp knitting needles, or size needed to knit gauge. Yarn needle for finishing.

Gauge: 7 sts = 1 inch in Fleur-de-lis (used on the palm and outside of thumb). Note: in order to get 7 sts to the inch in Waves as well, *do not* catch up the alternate color on leaps of only 4 sts. The knitting may be a little ridgy, but not in a bad way. You can steam the mitten lightly with an iron afterward.

Size: Man's large.

Patterns: Follow the graphs exactly. Fleur-de-lis is a multiple of 4 sts and 6 rounds. Waves is a multiple of 12 sts and 24 rounds, and hence rather awkward for small projects like mittens.

Note: Be sure to catch up the other strand behind your work when color changes are more than 4 sts apart. To see how to do this and to get other pointers on double-knitting, read General Instructions for Double Knitting before starting this project.

Cuff: On Can. no. 10 (U.S. no. 3) dp knitting needles and using lt yarn, cast on 44 sts. K 3, p 1 for 26 rounds. Then, k 1 round plain, adding 2 sts between the 3 k sts of each rib by knitting the loop between sts. Total: 68 sts. Arrange these sts so that there are 35 on the first needle, 17 on the second and 14 on the third. The second and third needles will be the palm, and the end of the round will be between the palm and the back of the hand.

Start pattern: Follow the graphs for both the palm and the back.

Start thumb gore in the first round: For the left mitten the first 5 sts of the second needle, and for the right mitten the last 5 sts of the third needle, form the base of the thumb gore. K the first and the last of these 5 sts in dk as markers, and inc by knitting both colors into them so that the lt st is added on the thumb gore side of the markers.

Inc within these lines 7 times for a total 17 sts within (but not including) the dk lines. Then, k straight up in pattern until 25 rounds above the cuff. Take thumb gore sts off onto a string. Cast on

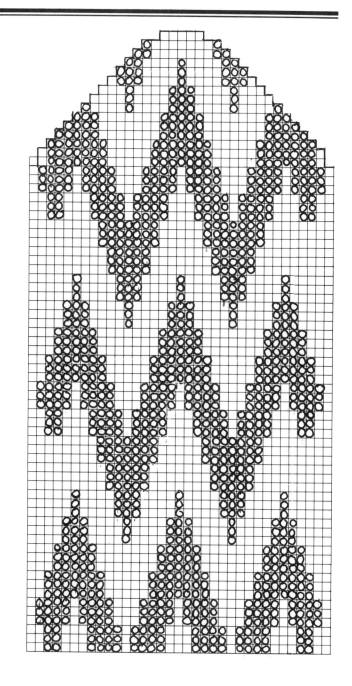

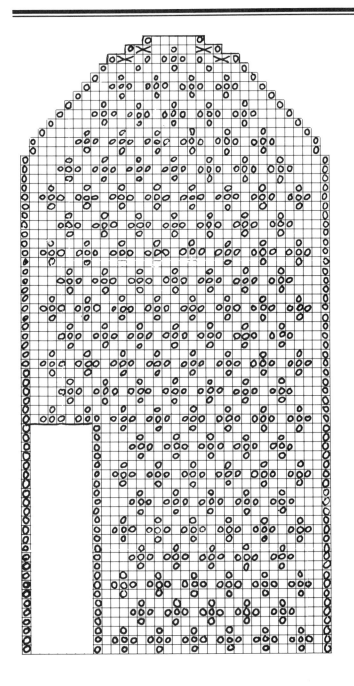

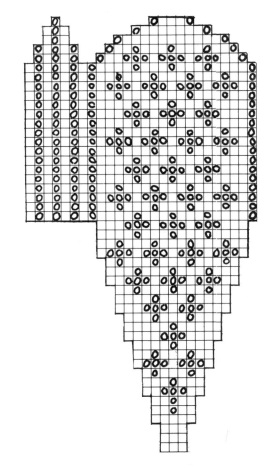

Left: Fleur-de-lis pattern for palm. Above: Stripes pattern runs up the inside of the thumb; rest of thumb is knit in Fleur-de-lis.

7 over the gap, in pattern, and continue knitting the hand until the dec point as shown on the graph.

Dec: First needle, slip first st, k 1 st, pass the slipped st over the k st. K up to the second st from the end of needle; k 2 together. At the beginning of second needle: k 1 dk, slip 1 st, k 1 st, pass the slipped st over the knitted st. K across the palm.

At end of the third needle, k up to 3 sts before the end. K 2 together. Dec this way every round, then where a 2-st-per-round dec is shown, k 2 together twice in the lt areas on both sides of the mitten in each round, while continuing to dec on the edges as before.

When about 10 sts remain, break the yarn. With a yarn needle, pull the lt yarn through the remaining sts and draw up tightly. Darn neatly across the tip in lt yarn. Draw both ends inside the mitten.

Thumb: Pick up on 2 needles the 17 sts from the string. On a third needle, pick up and k 9 sts from the back and corners of the thumb holes. These sts should be 1 dk, 1 lt across and ending with a dk st picked up from dk line that was a thumb gore marker. K straight up in vertical stripes on the inside of the thumb, and in Fleur-de-lis on the outside of the thumb.

(The striped inside surface of the thumb is characteristic of all Mrs. Montague's mittens. She was amused at a striped Maine mitten: ''She did it all like a thumb,'' she exclaimed. The stripes give a firmer fabric at this point of great wear.)

K straight up with Fleur-de-lis on the outside of the thumb and single-st stripes on the inside until the thumb is 2½ inches long. Dec as on the hand.

Draw all the tails to the inside, and finish by darning them into the inside surface of the mitten.

Double Irish Chain

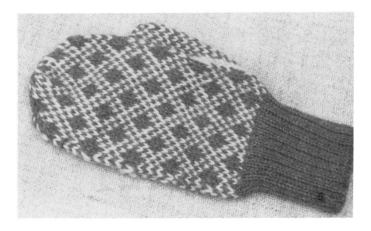

Double Irish Chain comes from Conception Harbour near St. John's, Newfoundland. Newfoundland folklorist Jerry Pocius reports that it's a common pattern in that area and is hooked into rugs and worked into patchwork quilts as well as knitted into mittens.

There is no way of knowing which came first, as the pattern works equally well in all three media, and we can only guess from the name that an Irish woman may have brought it here.

Double Irish Chain as I have knit it uses diamonds, like many Newfoundland and Labrador patterns, but doesn't tie them together into a check as is most common. Similar patterns of diamonds surrounded by "netting" are knitted in the British Isles and Scandinavia. Another one in this book is Fleur-de-lis and Diamonds, and even the Fleur-de-lis pattern itself could be considered a fat net separating little spaces, if you look at it with different eyes.

Double Irish Chain may also be knitted with the diamond seven stitches wide, optionally with a little prick in the center. I liked the look of the dark diamonds and the white chains, and so opted for the five-stitch diamond.

Like most double-knitting, in Newfoundland especially, Double Irish Chain is usually made with gray and white homespun (real homespun) yarns. I've knitted it here in rose and off-white Brunswick Pomfret sport yarn, a medium-weight fingering. Consider reversing light and dark on this pattern for a different look, but always carry the contrast color ahead.

This pattern may be substituted for the back pattern in any set of Labrador/Newfoundland instructions in this book: Tiny Diamonds, Mrs. Martin's Finger Mitts, Labrador Diamonds, or Shepherd's Plaid Gloves. There are eight stitches and eight rounds per pattern element, but this doesn't affect the structure of the mitten, because it's used only on the back, with Salt and Pepper on the thumb and palm.

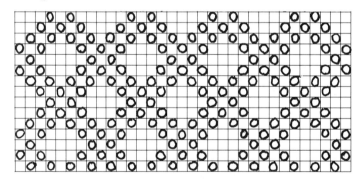

However, it might be fun to cover a whole mitten with this simple geometric pattern in the New Brunswick/Nova Scotia/Maine tradition. Check Fleur-de-lis and Diamonds pattern for sizes, and substitute Irish Chain for the pattern. Both patterns have 8-stitch elements.

—R.H.

Labrador Snowflake Mittens

Why is it that the most attractive arts are also the most inaccessible? Cree bead applique, Cherokee and Pomo basketmaking, Bluegrass fiddle playing—and Norwegian mitten making. Everywhere, people thirst after patterns, instructions, sheet music, for these arts. But when they find them, the notes produce something insipid, and the patterns produce a simplified stereotype.

The sheet music for "Dueling Banjos" (which I once yearned to play on the guitar) is an exception. It has large gaps, empty measures, above which is printed merely, "Improvise"! That helps me not at all, because I don't know mountain guitar pickin', and you will think that telling you to improvise Norwegian-style mittens in a Labrador tradition is no help either. But improvisation is the secret of all these crafts—Indian basket making and bead applique, mountain music and making mittens in a Norwegian or Labrador tradition.

Many of the knitters of both Scandinavian and

Newfoundland Labrador mitts regard yarn and knitting needles as an artistic medium and would no more think of following a written pattern than an artist would use a paint-by-number canvas. The emphasis is on improvisation. If you look closely, you'll see that even the photo and diagram show some variations. Choose the alternatives you like best—or, better yet, design your own.

Nora Johnson, of Georgetown, Maine, who knits Fox and Geese, Striped, and Salt and Pepper mittens told me, "I try to make a perfect mitten." What she meant by perfect is that it must look right in every particular. Although these appear to be three of the simpler double-knit mittens, she often pulls out and reknits, redesigns thumbs or final closures until her skill and design sense permeates every stitch, and the mitten is perfect. Given one of my written patterns to try, she redesigned the decreases so that the mitten ended with a little pinwheel in the contrasting color. Mitten knitting can be an art, requiring creativity, and the mittens of Labrador and Scandinavia are just that.

However, I will give you some guidelines, so you'll be one step ahead of me in my attempts to play "Dueling Banjos."

All the mittens with large motifs shown here are more or less improvisations or variations on a theme by someone. She may never have made the same mitten again. But they must be planned out ahead of time, because (1) you have a limited five-sided shape to cover with what is traditionally a quad-ratically symmetrical design, and (2) you must avoid both long leaps between color changes and rounds with only one or no contrasting stitches on the back. Another reason to plan ahead is because it's psychologically easier to erase an X on graph paper than it is to rip out half a mitten.

In these mittens, the basic shapes are big stars (or snowflakes) and flowers. (A graphed flower is found in the Shining Star instructions.) The main difference between these is that flowers are rounded at the corners, while the stars/snowflakes are pointed.

Into the hollows between the points of the stars are put lines, crosses, feathery things, edges of flowers, or simple geometric shapes, either solid, or in a one-one alternation.

The palms will be familiar if you've already knit any Maine or Atlantic Canadian patterns: they are usually knit in Salt and Pepper, Fleur-de-lis, or any small pattern. Forget the palms for now.

Size is controlled by (1) the size of the star, etc., (2) what's added around the star, and (3) what's added around the entire graphed pattern. Some of the stars are large enough to contain a second star in the main color. The Shining Star pattern has a small star but lots of "feathers." Some of the Labrador Snowflake instructions call for adding an edge outside the design—two main color and one contrasting color stitches—which widens the mitten by putting a border between the front and the back. These edges can be a simple line or two, or an extension of the background for two or three stitches. Fancier versions may be a vertical three- to five-stitch band decorated with a single dot every other round, or a simple design like Fleur-de-lis or Spruce (see diagram).

Basically, one takes a mitten pattern and splits the number of stitches—half for the palm, half for the back. Then get a piece of graph paper with fairly small squares and go at it, within the tradition that interests you. Use my snowflakes if you like. Use someone else's. But adapt them to the space you need to fill.

Usually no one but a skinny, true Scandinavian has a hand that's long enough to accommodate two snowflakes or stars on top of each other unless there's been some widening at the edges. The light brown example is really too long for a small woman's hand, but too narrow (and the thumb is too low) for a medium woman's hand. (Do Scandinavians have low thumbs? Did the Inuit woman who knit the mitten have a low thumb?)

Small or wide hands may require only a pattern and a half. Decide ahead whether you want the half pattern at the tip of the mitten or at the base next to the cuff. Should it be the same or something entirely different? Maybe you want the main pattern in the middle with partial patterns on both ends. Experiment; the product will be yours alone.

Plan **ahead** of time where you're going to cut a pattern. The left mitten is not as attractive as the right one. The star on the left mitten might not even show beneath a coat sleeve. Notice also the advantage of spacing the stars a row apart so the light-colored twigs at the corners of the stars don't merge into a nondescript geometric shape.

If you want to plan your mitten from start to finish before knitting the cuff, you would do well to make a tubular swatch (you can use it for a doll hat) about 24 stitches around and about two inches long in something like Fleur-de-lis to find out how many stitches and how many rounds you knit per inch.

Measure the wearer's hand from the base of the palm to the base of the fingernail on the ring finger, multiply by the number of rounds you knit per inch, and you'll know the point where the decrease begins. After that point, you will decrease every round (four stitches per round, counting the palm) for these mittens. That's the tradition. It makes the end look like a housetop. At the very end, you can sneak in more decreases to make it a little bit less pointed, so leave space (background) in your graphed pattern for this to happen and mark it by taking off two stitches, instead of one, at the edges, even though you actually will put these extra decreases in the middle of the rows.

For the thumb, you have great latitude. You can make a thumb that's just Salt and Pepper. You can make a mitten with or without a thumb gore, and with the thumb gore decorated or plain. The Labrador Snowflake mittens here have reasonable widths for goreless mittens, and most of the other mitten patterns in this book will give a fair idea of how much to add, and when, for a thumb gore.

For gloves, try either improvising on Janetta's pattern for Flying Geese gloves—which have to be the most comfortable man's glove ever knit—or the Shepherd's Plaid, which use a coarser yarn.

For those whom Elizabeth Zimmermann calls "blind followers," which usually includes me, I have given instructions for a simple, goreless mitten. They follow.

—R.H.

Labrador Snowflake Mittens

Materials: 2 to 3 ounces each lt and dk, lightweight worsted yarn. Briggs and Little 2/12 was used for the example. Brunswick Yarns Germantown, Bartlettyarns 2-ply Fisherman Yarn, or other lightweight worsteds can be substituted.

Equipment: One set Can. no. 10 (U.S. no. 3) dp knitting needles, or size needed to knit Salt and Pepper pattern to gauge. Yarn needle for finishing.

Gauge: 7 sts = 1 inch.

Sizes: Child's 2 to 3 years (child's 4 to 6, child's 8 to 10, woman's medium, man's medium). Man's large is not suited to this pattern. Use Shining Star or Waves.

Patterns: Snowflake and Salt-and-Pepper.

Snowflake is a multiple of 21, 25, or 31 sts and rounds, depending on size. Snowflake is knitted only once for gloves and repeated once and a half to twice on mittens, one immediately joining the one before.

For the palm, Salt and Pepper, a simple one-one alternation of the two colors. The second round is reversed from the first.

The contrasting color should be carried ahead at all times.

Please read General Instructions for Double-Knitting and the introduction to this pattern before starting on this project.

Cuff: Using main color (mc), cast on 30 (36, 42, 48,

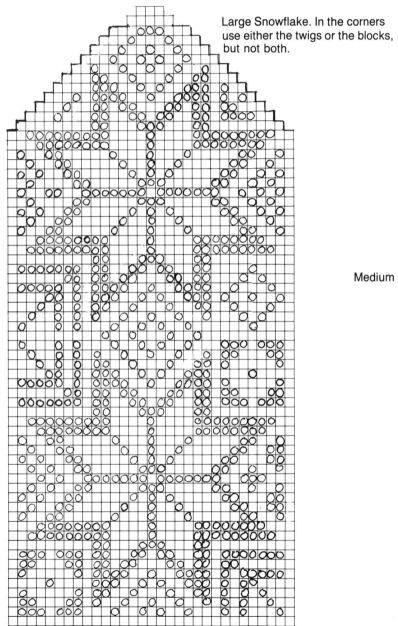

Large Snowflake. In the corners
use either the twigs or the blocks,
but not both.

Medium Snowflake.

Small Snowflake.

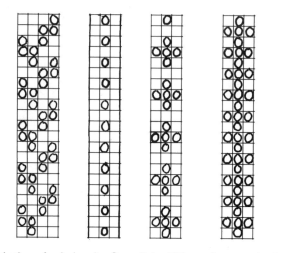

Edge designs for Labrador Snowflake Mittens: leaves, single dot, Fleur-de-lis, Spruce.

54) sts. K 2, p 1 for 18 (21, 23, 26, 29) rounds, putting in a stripe after 6 (7, 9, 10, 10) rounds as follows: K 1 round contrasting color (cc), k 1 round mc until there are 4 or 5 cc stripes forming a broad band. Finish cuff in mc.

Change to stockinette st, k 1 round in mc, increasing in the loops between the two k sts in each rib 10 (12, 13, 14, 16) times. You may have to add 1 or 2 more sts than the number of loops between k sts to get a total of 42 (49, 55, 62, 70) sts. Do this in the first pattern round by knitting both colors into 1 st, in the correct order for the pattern.

Rearrange sts on the needles so that half the sts are on the third needle and one-quarter are on each of the other 2 needles. The first st of the round should still be at the beginning of the first needle, and there should be an uneven number of sts on the third needle, namely, 21 (25, 27, 31, 35). The third needle will be the back of the mitten; the other two will be the palm.

Start patterns: K Salt and Pepper on the first and second needles.

On the third needle begin the graphed pattern. For child's size 2 to 3 use the small pattern. For size 4 to 6 use the small pattern but add 1 more st in mc and 1 st in cc to both sides.

For child's size 8 to 10 and woman's medium, use the middle-sized pattern. For 8 to 10, add one more st in mc to both sides. For women's medium, add 2 more mc sts and 1 cc st on each side of the graph—or use the large pattern, which fits exactly horizontally, and start halfway up, at the center of the snowflake.

For man's medium, use the large pattern and add one more mc st and one cc st on each side of the graphed pattern to make a line up the sides. Start the pattern at the middle, going up.

There is no thumb gore. K straight up in these patterns for 9 (11, 13, 15, 15) rounds.

For the left mitten, the thumb hole is on the first 8 (8, 10, 10, 12) sts of the first needle. For the right mitten, it's on the last 8 (8, 10, 10, 12) sts of the second needle. K a separate contrasting bit of yarn (not cc) into these sts, then backtrack and reknit them in pattern. (You will pick out the marking strand later, pick up the sts it joined, add sts in the corners, and have enough sts to make a thumb.) Continue to k straight up in the Snowflake and Salt and Pepper patterns until the mitten is 3 (3½, 4½, 5½, 6) inches above the cuff.

Hand dec (if you reach the correct measure and haven't quite finished the second snowflake, dec anyhow, convincing yourself you planned it that way): At the beginning of the first needle, k 2 together, knitting into the back of both sts to maintain the cc line up the side, if you have one.

K to 2 sts from the end of the second needle.
K 2 together, in pattern. Third needle: k 2 together,
knitting into the back of the sts. Knit to 3 sts from
end and k 2 together before the cc line. Move the
cc st to the third needle and k it together with the
next st, knitting into the back of both sts. Dec this
way every round until you run out of pattern on
the back of the hand and are down to about 16 sts.
Then k 2 together twice on both the front and the
back in the mc, while continuing to dec as before.
When only about 9 sts remain, break the yarn,
draw up the remaining sts on the cc, and darn the
cc strand back and forth across the tip.

Thumb: Pick out the contrasting marker strand and
pick up 8 (8, 10, 10, 12) sts from the bottom of the
thumb hole on 2 needles. Pick up the little loops
(the same number as on the bottom) along the top
of the thumb hole. Now, k 1 st into the outside
corner, k across the back of the thumb hole in Salt
and Pepper pattern, k 2 sts into the corner of the
thumb hole on the palm side, then k the sts along
the bottom of the thumb hole. If you are bothered
by the top of the mitten flopping in your face while
you're knitting the thumb, tuck the top into the
cuff, inside out, to get it out of the way.

K straight up in Salt and Pepper for 1¼ (1½, 2, 2¼,
2½) inches. You will have an uneven number of sts,
so don't worry about changing the alternation every
round; it will do itself. Dec just as for hand until
6 to 8 sts remain. Break yarn and pull the remainder
up on the cc end, and darn it back and forth neatly
over the tip.

Draw all ends into the mitten, turn it inside out,
and darn down all the ends. Tighten up any loose
sts at the beginning of the thumb at this time too.

Shining Star Mitts
from Saint Anthony's

Shining Star Mitt, on right.

This pattern, an eight-pointed star with fernlike leaves or rays extending out from four corners, is one of the most common of large Norwegian motifs and is found in almost identical versions on both sides of the Atlantic. The mitten I copied came from Phyllis Montague, of Northwest River, Labrador— the same Mrs. Montague who gave me the Big Waves pattern. Both mittens were knitted for her as patterns by her mother, of St. Anthony's, Newfoundland. Both were larger than most human hands, knit at about seven stitches per inch.

Possibly her mother wanted to give her the design at its fullest, so that smaller mittens could be made by cutting off outside portions of the motifs, or perhaps the mitten might originally have been knit tighter—say at eight, nine, or ten stitches per inch— considerably reducing its size. As is, this pattern makes a man's large very nicely, knitted at seven stitches per inch.

I have successfully decreased its size both ways. I've decreased the number of stitches by taking four off both sides of both the palm and the back, and I've tightened the gauge by using a light worsted weight (such as Briggs & Little 2/12) yarn on U.S. no. 2 (Can. no. 11) needles at a tension of eight stitches to an inch. The resultant fabric is dense and smooth; the cuff, the most elastic I've ever knit—all in all, a rewarding experiment.

If you opt to decrease the width by cutting off stitches, you will have to decrease the length as well. I cut off the lacy ruffle around the flower, for which there wouldn't have been enough width across anyhow.

A tension of eight stitches to the inch is handy for sizing, as each stitch equals ⅛ inch. By taking 1 stitch off each edge, front and back, you take off a half-inch in width, which happens to be the difference between most of the sizes. However, I will leave this game to you, and I don't recommend that you try cutting stitches off the graph for this mitten until you have played with a few other double-knit patterns.

Phyllis Montague's mother drafted out where things will fall by alternating dark and light in the first round after the cuff. All the major points of the ensuing pattern rise above these little dots, including the fleurs-de-lis on the palm.

Big Waves and Shining Star are almost the same mitten but with different designs on the back. The main difference is that this pattern decreases every round all the way up the tip, giving it a housetop look compared to the rounded tip of Big Waves.

Please don't be alarmed if you make small mistakes. Counting out stitches on at least 25 of these Norwegian-style mittens has convinced me that the only perfect ones are in the minds of their creators

Palm and thumb detail.

and the eyes of their beholders. Generally speaking, the human eye corrects small irregularities in geometric patterns. Even with some errors, these are spectacular mittens—and a mistake or two proves they were made by human hands. (Machines only make big mistakes.) Can you find *my* errors on the back? On the palm?

—R.H.

Shining Star Mitts

Materials: about 3 ounces each of dk and lt worsted weight yarn. While in Norway these mittens might be knitted in a bright color or black and white, Newfoundland/Labrador knitters tend to use natural sheep colors—grays, browns, and natural white—or the heathery colors from Briggs & Little.

Equipment: If knitting the tighter gauge (for women's medium), use 1 set U.S. no. 1 (Can. no. 13) dp knitting needles for the cuff and 1 set U.S. no. 2 (Can. no. 11) for the main part of the mitten, or whatever size you need to get that gauge. If knitting the looser gauge (for man's large), use 1 set U.S. no. 2 (Can. no. 11) dp knitting needles for the cuff and 1 set U.S. no. 3 (Can. no. 10) for the body of the mitten, or whatever size you need for that gauge.

Gauge: 8 sts = 1 inch in Fleur-de-lis, or 7 sts = 1 inch in Fleur-de-lis.

Sizes: At 8 sts = 1 inch, woman's medium. At 7 sts = 1 inch, man's medium to large.

Patterns: Shining Star and Fleur-de-lis.

Shining Star, a typical large Norwegian motif, is 35 sts wide as graphed. (To make other sizes than those presented, it's fairly easy to reduce the width by eliminating 2 sts on each side of both front and palm for each size smaller. Figure how to reduce the length at the same time—before you start knitting.)

Fleur-de-lis is a common palm pattern on mittens like these. It's a multiple of 4 sts and 6 rounds.

Stripes, used on the inside of all Mrs. Montague's thumbs, is her own touch. Most Norwegian-style knitters extend the palm pattern onto the inside of the thumb and have a different pattern on the outside of the thumb.

Note: Do not be alarmed by the hole for the thumb in the palm graph. It's there only because it's impossible to graph palm and thumb in the same space. When you knit, simply insert the first round of the thumb graph into the first round of the hole.

Please read General Instructions for Double Knitting before starting on this project.

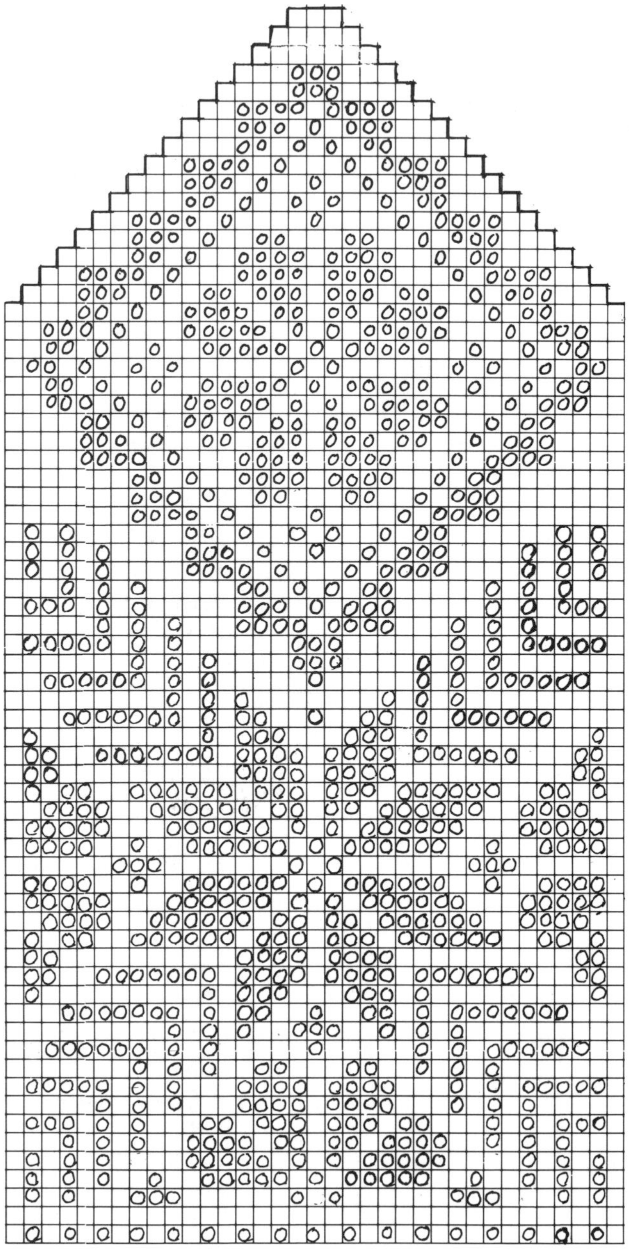

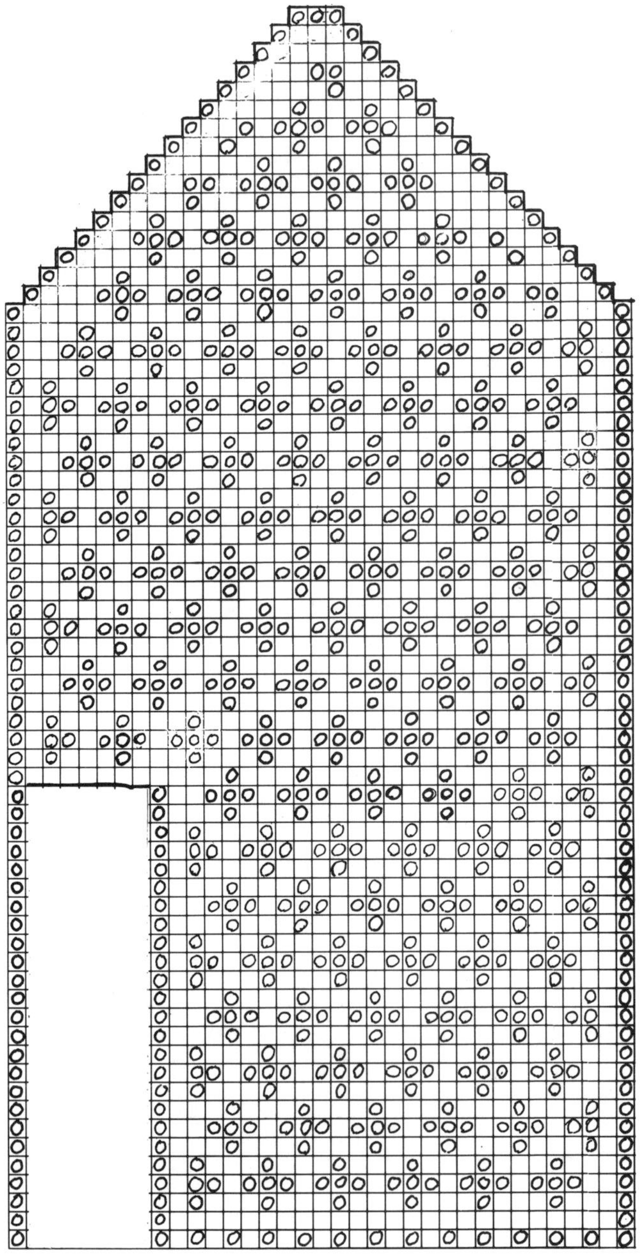

On three of the smaller size needles and using dk yarn, cast on 44 sts. K 3, p 1 for 26 rounds, knitting contrasting horizontal stripes after 9 rounds, if you wish.

Change to larger needles and k 1 round in dk, adding 2 sts between the 3 k sts of each rib by lifting and knitting into the loop between sts, to make a total of 66 sts. For the left mitten, arrange these sts so that there are 35 on the first needle, 17 on the second, and 14 on the third. The first needle will be the back, and the end of the round will change between the palm and the back of the hand. The needle with 14 sts will have the thumb gore in the last 5 sts.

Start thumb gore in the first round: Either the first 5 sts of the second needle (right mitten) or the last 5 sts of the third needle (left mitten), form the base of the thumb gore. K the first and the last of these 5 sts in lt as markers, and inc by knitting both colors into them so that the dk st is added on the thumb-gore side of the markers.

Also in the first row, start pattern: Follow the graphs precisely, especially in the first few rounds until you get the lines established.

At the thumb hole, take off and put on a string all the sts between the 2 lt lines, but not the marking lines themselves. There should be 17 sts. Cast on 7 over the hole and continue to follow the graph straight up. When you reach the little dot beneath the ruffled frame around the flower, you have a decision to make: If the hand you are knitting for is a long woman's hand or a large man's hand, ignore the little dot and continue following the graph. If the hand is a medium man's or an ordinary medium woman's, start the ruffled frame at the dot, mentally pulling the frame down closer into the graph.

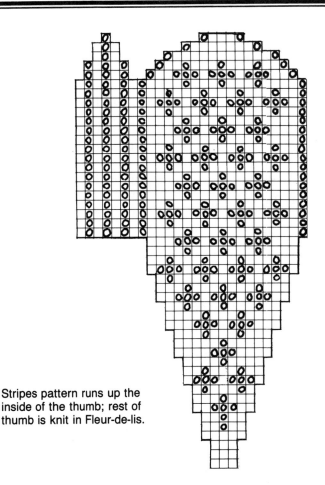

Stripes pattern runs up the inside of the thumb; rest of thumb is knit in Fleur-de-lis.

Make the decreases as shown on the graphs, on the palm as well, decreasing 1 st each round at each point. To make the dec slant properly at the beginning of the front and the palm, read the dec instructions in General Instructions for Double Knitting. If you still need more length, you can put off beginning the dec for 2 or 3 rounds.

When only about 6 to 8 sts remain at the tip, break the yarn, thread one tail onto a yarn needle, and pull up the remaining sts firmly on it. Darn neatly

back and forth across the tip, concealing your sts
in sts of the right color. Do the same with the other
tail, then pull them inside.

Thumb: Using three needles, pick up the 17 sts of
the thumb gore and 9 sts from the top and corners
of the thumb hole in the correct colors to continue
knitting the Fleur-de-lis pattern on the outside and
Stripes on the inside. The 2 lt sts forming the
outside edges of the thumb gore will continue up
the sides of the thumb, becoming the outermost lt
stripe on the inside of the thumb. Follow the graph
to the tip, then finish as you did the hand.

Draw all tails to the inside and darn them to the
inside surface of the mitten, hiding the ends under
loops of the opposite color.

You've just completed the left mitten. Don't forget,
when you're arranging sts for the *right* mitten, that
the 14-st needle will be the third needle and that
the thumb will begin at the end of that needle.
You wouldn't want 2 left mittens.

Two Traditional Caps with Double-knit Patterns

If you have traditional double-knit mittens, it's nice to have at least a hat to go with them. Some people also like to knit socks and sweaters to match, but maybe that's carrying it too far. These two caps are designs I've seen in Newfoundland and Maine.

There are two reasonable places to put a double-knit design on a cap—on the crown and on the turned-up cuff. You can apply any of the small geometric patterns to either of these caps, but think a little about the pattern first. Very small patterns look better on the crown, and big or blocky patterns look good both places, but great on the cuff.

—R.H.

A French Canadian Toque

This cap has the pattern on the turned-up cuff. That means you have to work either the design in purl or the crown in purl, as the cuff must be turned up, and if you knit both, the cuff will end up inside out.

Materials: 3 ounces dk, 2 ounces lt worsted weight yarn.

Equipment: 1 set U.S. no. 5 (Can. no. 8) dp knitting needles for ribbing; 1 set U.S. no. 8 (Can. no. 5) dp knitting needles, or size needed to knit correct gauge. Yarn needle for finishing.

Gauge: 5½ sts = 1 inch in pattern. 5 sts = 1 inch in plain stockinette st.

Sizes: Child's 1 to 3 (child's 3 to 6, adult). This corresponds to a final cap width of 16 (18, 20) inches. The circumference of a knitted cap should be from 2 to 4 inches less than the actual head measurement.

Pattern: Find the adult mitten pattern for the design you want to use. Divide the number of sts per pattern element into the number of sts in the size cap you want to knit and adjust the number so that you can knit complete pattern elements. Remember that it's better for a hat to be a little small rather than floppy loose.

Be sure to read General Instructions for Double-Knitting before starting this project.

Starting from the cuff and using the larger needles, cast on 90 (100, 108) sts. Change to the smaller needles and k 1, p 1 for 4 rounds.

Change back to larger needles and *purl* pattern for 12 to 16 rounds, whatever works with your pattern. (If you're using Compass, be sure to have a contrasting line both top and bottom.) Carry the yarn-not-in-use on the side of knit that faces you.

Change to the smaller needles and k 1, p 1 for 9 rounds.

Change to larger needles and stockinette st. K 2 together 8 (6, 8) times, evenly spaced. K straight up for 4¼ (4½, 4¾) inches.

Dec: K 10, k 2 together, repeating around.

K 2 rounds.

K 9, k 2 together, around.

K 2 rounds.

K 8, k 2 together around.

K 2 rounds.

Continue to dec this way every other round with fewer sts between decs each time until you k 1, k 2 together around. Continue to k 1, k 2 together every round until only about 32 sts remain.

Break the yarn, leaving a tail about 8 inches long. Thread the tail through the remaining sts with a yarn needle and draw them up firmly. Draw the tail through the remaining sts twice more, then darn back and forth over the tip to reinforce it. Work all ends into the back of the fabric.

A Double-knit Cap

The pattern on this cap is on the crown. It's a cap seen in Newfoundland but rarely in other parts of the area, where caps are usually knit in one-color ribbing.

Materials: 2 to 3 ounces dk and 1 to 2 ounces lt worsted weight wool yarn.

Equipment: 1 set 10-inch U.S. no. 7 (Can. no. 6) dp or straight knitting needles, or size needed to knit your choice of pattern in correct gauge. 1 set 10-inch U.S. no. 4 (Can. no. 9) dp or straight knitting needles for ribbed cuff. Yarn needle for finishing.

Gauge: 6 sts = 1 inch in pattern.

Sizes: Child's small (child's medium, adult's medium, adult's large), corresponding to a cap measuring 16 (18, 20, 22) inches around. For a good fit, caps should be 2 to 4 inches smaller than the circumference of the head.

Pattern: See the adult mitten pattern in the design you want to knit for graph and pattern notes. To determine the correct number of sts to cast on, divide the number of sts in your pattern element into the number of sts given for the size cap you want to knit. Choose the closest number that lets you knit complete pattern elements.

If working flat, purl every other row and read the pattern left to right on purl rows. Add 1 more st to both ends for the seam.

Please read General Instructions for Double Knitting before starting this project.

Cuff: On smaller needles, cast on 96 (108, 120, 132) sts in dk. K 1, p 1 for 3 (3½, 4, 4) inches.

Change to larger needles and start pattern, adding sts here if necessary to make your pattern come out even. K straight up in pattern for 3¾ (4½, 5, 5) inches.

Adjust sts so that there is roughly the same number on each needle. Dec at both ends of all three needles by knitting 2 sts together (or whatever dec method is suggested for the tip of the matching mittens), but dec 1 at each end of each needle at these 3 points.

K 4 (4, 5, 5) rounds in pattern.

Repeat dec round.

K 2 (2, 3, 3) rounds.

Repeat dec round.

K 1 (1, 2, 2) rounds in pattern.

Repeat dec round, then k every round as a dec round until only 18 sts remain.

Break yarn and pull up remaining sts firmly on both strands. Thread the tails through these sts once more, then darn each strand individually into the inside of the tip. Work all other loose ends into the back of the fabric.

Attach a single- or two-colored pompom to the tip, if it strikes your fancy.

The cuff should be turned up about half its length, so that it also forms the inside band of the cap.

Part Three

Chicky Feet: Double-knits for Babies and Small Children

Baby mittens: (back row) Double Irish Chain (use directions for Tiny Labrador Diamonds), Partridge Chicky Feet, Chipman's Block; (front row) Tiny Labrador Diamonds, Compass, Petites Mitaines en Fleur-de-lis, and Cunnin' Old-timey Baby Mittens.

Here are some of the same traditional patterns knit with a gentler yarn for babies and children up to four years old—at least one pattern for each of the regions and groups in the adult section. The two layers of yarn and the tightness of the knit make a very warm but light garment.

For little babies these can be knit with synthetic yarn, as it's unlikely they will spend much time in wet snow.

They use sizes 2, 3, and 4 double-pointed needles and, except for the Cunnin' Old-timey Baby Mittens, are quickly made. The yarn is medium-weight fingering, or sport yarn, a little thicker than baby yarn.

These sizes overlap the sizes of the worsted weight mittens at size 2 to 4. The worsted weight is more quickly knit and heavier, but is also bulkier, like new denim blue jeans in babies' sizes.

Cunnin' Old-timey Baby Mittens

These little mittens are a copy of a tiny pair shown to me in Brunswick, Maine, by a woman whose family had saved them for several generations. I never learned her name, and have not been able to find her again, but I remember the mittens very well. They were knit in soft green and white, probably in a mixture of silk and wool, although maybe of silk alone. They were knit in incredibly small stitches, probably impossible to duplicate today without manufacturing your own needles.

The striped pattern tends to pull up the fabric, making the knit even tighter than would normally be knit on a given size needle.

The beauty of such a fine gauge is the thinness, the softness, the firmness of the resultant fabric, and that I have almost duplicated in my copy.

These little mittens are knit on size 2 needles, but at a tension of 10.5 stitches per inch. This means they will take a good knitter several hours to knit, but it shouldn't discourage even a beginner from making them. The pattern is simple, the increases and decreases are of an elementary sort, and (fortunately) the mittens are tiny.

The pattern on the cuff, Peek-a-boo, is common in Nova Scotia and is used in the Hebrides and Fair Isle as a cuff stitch. Like Chipman's Block, it is an alternation of 3 light, 3 dark, with rounds of 1 light, 1 dark. Often the simple things are best.

—R.H.

Cunnin' Old-timey Baby Mittens

Materials: About ¾ ounce off-white and ¾ ounce colored sport weight yarn. Brunswick Yarns Pomfret was used in the example.

Equipment: 1 set U.S. no. 2 dp needles (Can. no. 11), or size needed to k pattern to gauge. This size is also used for the cuff. Yarn needle for finishing.

Gauge: An incredible 10.5 sts = 1 inch. Happily, the mittens are small.

Sizes: 6 months to 1 year. Instructions for 18 months to 2 years and 3 to 4 years are given in parentheses.

Patterns: Peek-a-boo and Stripes. Peek-a-boo, a multiple of 6 sts and 6 rounds is used on the cuff.

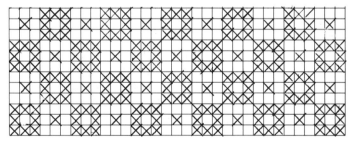

First round: K 3 dk, k 3 lt around.

Second round: K 1 dk, k 1 lt around.

Third round: K 3 dk, k 3 lt around.

Fourth round: K 3 lt, k 3 dk around.

Fifth round: K 1 lt, k 1 dk around.

Sixth round: K 3 lt, k 3 dk around.

Stripes is a 2-st alternation of 2 colors, which pulls the knit up in ridges, making a tighter fabric than is possible with a single color. To make the dk color stand out, as in the example, carry it ahead of the light yarn. All rounds: K 1 dk, k 1 lt around on an even number of sts.

Read General Instructions for Double Knitting before starting this project.

Cuff: Using the Maine method and dk yarn, cast on 48 (54, 60) sts. Begin Peek-a-boo pattern immediately, carrying the dk color ahead. K 4 bands of Peek-a-boo.

Change to Stripes pattern. Inc for the thumb gore, starting in the first round, by knitting both colors into the last 2 sts. K 1 more round in pattern, then inc 4 sts, 2 each in the last dk stripe of the third needle and in the first dk stripe on the first needle (transfer this to the third needle). Read below how to inc in Stripes.

Inc: K into the dk st in the row below, directly under the one you would ordinarily k into, and use both colors, dk then lt. Then k the st above in dk. This should make a little dk Y with a lt st in the middle.

For size 3 to 4, k 3 more rounds and repeat this inc in the 2 dk stripes now on the outer edges of the thumb gore. There are no more incs.

K straight up in pattern until 1 (1¼, 1½) inches above cuff. Put on a string or safety pin the thumb gore sts plus the 2 lt sts just outside the thumb gore—that is, 11 (11, 15) sts. Cast on 5 sts over the gap in pattern—3 lt and 2 dk. The pattern will fit with the rest of the mitten.

K straight up in pattern 1¾ (2, 2¼) inches.

Now, arrange sts with 15 (17, 19) on two needles and 16 (18, 18) on the third, and so that one needle covers most of the back of the hand. Each needle should begin with a dk st.

Dec: In first round, k 1 dk, k 1 lt, k 1 dk and 1 lt together in dk, k 1 dk, k 1 lt, and continue up to 4 sts before end of needle. K 1 dk and 1 lt together in dk; k 1 dk, k 1 lt. (You will have dk sts together at each end of the needle.) Repeat this on all three needles.

Second round: On each needle, k 1 dk and 1 lt together in dk, and k the next st (which is dk) in lt. K 1 dk, k 1 lt up to 3 sts before end of needle, then k 1 dk, k 1 dk and 1 lt together in lt.

The idea is to keep the dk lines dominant all the way to the tip of the fingers.

After you've done this once or twice, it will make sense, but don't despair if you've forgotten it by the next time you make a striped mitten. I have to check my own instructions every time.

Repeat these 2 rounds until about 6 sts remain. Break yarn. Draw lt yarn into the mitten. Draw remaining sts up firmly on the dk tail, then darn it invisibly back and forth across the tip a few times.

Thumb: Pick up on 2 needles 11 (11, 15) sts from the string. Pick up on the third needle 9 sts from the back and corners—one in each of the 5 sts on the back and 2 dk in the dk stripes on the sides.

You should have 2 dk together in each corner. Establish the alternating lt and dk stripe pattern by knitting both dk and lt into the first st in each of these dk pairs. You'll now have a total 22 (22, 26) sts.

K straight up 1 (1, 1¼) inches. Dec exactly as on hand until 6 sts remain. Finish as on hand.

With yarn needle, draw all tails into the mitten, turn it inside out, and darn all ends into the inside surface. Done.

Compass Mittens for Small Mariners

I first heard of Compass Mittens from a distant cousin on Bailey Island, one of Maine's Harpswell Islands. Later, Janetta Dexter showed me the pattern, occasionally knit in Nova Scotia and New Brunswick, which has a variety of names, including Mattie Owl's Patch.

In spite of the color of the Mattie Owl story, I still like "Compass Mittens" better, perhaps because it comes from my own people, the Harpswell islanders of 100 years ago. And I can always see compass needles pointing northward in the design. I knit this baby mitten in a navy blue and natural cream for people like myself, who want their babies to carry on the family's nautical tradition. Like many quilt designs, it offers young minds food for thought, directions to look to.

—R.H.

Compass Mittens for Small Mariners

Materials: ½ ounce each lt and dk sportweight (fingering, in Canada) yarn, preferably wool. Brunswick Yarns Pomfret was used for the example.

Equipment: 1 set U.S. no. 2 (Can. no. 11) dp knitting needles, or size needed to knit Compass pattern to gauge. 1 set U.S. no. 1 (Can. no. 13) dp knitting needles for ribbed cuff. Yarn needle for finishing.

Gauge: 9 sts = 1 inch in Compass pattern.

Sizes: Instructions are for size 6 months to 1 year. Instructions for 18 months to 2 years and 4 years are shown in parentheses. A true three-year-old size doesn't work unless you halve one pattern element all the way up. If you decide to improvise a 3-year-old size, calculate measurements midway between the second and third sizes given here, and put the halved pattern element on the palm side just before it merges into the back on the little-finger edge of the hand.

Pattern: Compass is a multiple of 8 rounds and 8 sts. (It can't be knit flat, unless one carries the second color behind when knitting the single-color round, and this isn't really worth the trouble.)

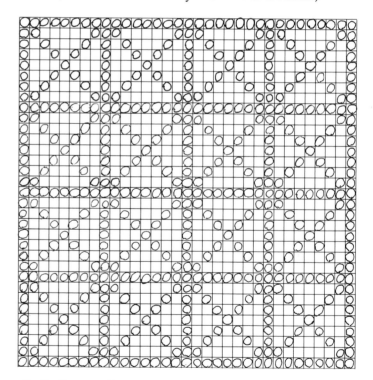

Cuff: On smaller needles, cast on 40 (48, 56) sts. K 3, p 1 in lt for 10 rounds, dk for 4 rounds, lt for 2 rounds, dk for 4 rounds, and lt for 7 rounds.

Change to larger needles and k 1 round in dk.

Then start pattern: You will have 5 (6, 7) 8-st pattern elements. K top half (whole, whole) band of pattern.

Start thumb gore: For the left mitten, the last 8 sts of the round form the base of the thumb gore. (For the right mitten, use the first 8 sts of the round.) At the first round of the second band of pattern, inc 6 sts within these 8 sts, all in the same round, by a combination of knitting both colors into 1 st and by looping the appropriate yarn between sts as if to knit.

Inc: K a st for the first upright (dk), then add 3 sts before the center st: *k both colors into the next st (dk then lt), loop lt yarn as if to k between sts, and knit both colors into the next st, lt then dk*. K the next upright in dk, then repeat * to *. You will now have 2 pattern elements above 1, both of them lacking a single st. Add this st in the next round, next to the uprights, by knitting both colors into 1 st so that it fits into the pattern. This is the only inc.

Complete band of pattern.

Take off for thumb: For right mitten, k 1, then put 15 sts on a safety pin. Cast on 7 sts over the gap. K straight up in pattern until 2¾ (3¼, 3¾) inches above the cuff.

Dec: K 2 together whenever there are 2 or more sts of 1 color together, around (but with at least 1 st between each dec in this round). Or k 1, k 2 together if you are in the all-dk round.

Next round, sort out your pattern as best you can, emphasizing the vertical lines wherever possible, and k in pattern around once without decs. Dec again in the next round and the next, then k 2 together around, alternating colors if that works, or all dk, if that fits into the design. You should

have about 12 to 14 sts left.

Break both strands, leaving 6-inch tails, and pull the dk tail through the remaining sts. Darn it back and forth over the tip, concealing your sts in the dk knitted sts. Then draw both tails into the mitten.

Thumb: Pick up 15 sts from thumb gore on 2 needles. On a third needle, pick up and k 9 sts from the back and corners. Total: 24 sts. This is rather a large thumb for the small sizes, so you can k the thumb on the same size needles as the cuff to make it narrower. K straight up in pattern for ¾ (1, 1¼) inches. Decrease either as you did on the hand or k 1, k 2 together around twice, matching colors to the pattern as best you can, until 6 to 8 sts remain. Finish as on hand.

Draw all remaining tails to the inside, darn them into the inside surface of the knit, and trim off the ends. Turn the mitten right side out, and make another.

Tiny Labrador Diamonds Mitts

Here are mitts in the Diamond, or Wave, pattern for little ones. I've left off the trigger finger and gloves, because fingers are usually a bother with such small children. Any of the Diamond patterns under Mrs. Martin's Finger Mitts or the small Wave pattern can be substituted for this pattern with no other adjustments.

—R.H.

Tiny Labrador Diamonds Mitts

Materials: About ½ ounce lt and ¾ ounce dk colored sportweight yarn (fingering yarn in Canada), preferably wool.

Equipment: 1 set U.S. no. 2 (Can. no. 11) dp knitting needles, or size needed to knit the pattern to gauge. 1 set U.S. no. 1 (Can. no. 13) dp knitting needles for ribbed cuff. Yarn needle for finishing.

Gauge: 9 sts = 1 inch in Salt and Pepper pattern.

Sizes: Instructions are for newborn to 6 months. Sizes 2, 3, and 4 are in parentheses.

Pattern: Any of the Diamond patterns can be used in place of the one shown here, or the small Wave pattern (see Mrs. Martin's Finger Mitts) for the back of the hand. All are multiples of 14 sts and have alternating dk and lt 7-st blocks. For the palm and thumb, use Salt and Pepper, a simple one-one alternation of lt and dk, which changes with each round.

Carry the dk color ahead.

Be sure to read General Instructions for Double Knitting before starting this project.

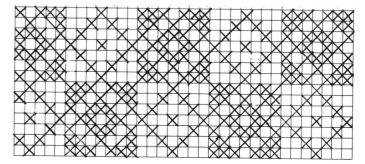

Cuff: On the smaller dp needles and with lt yarn, cast on 40 (48, 52, 56) sts. K 2, p 2 for 1½ (1¾, 2, 2¼) inches.

Change to larger needles. Rearrange sts so that half of them are divided between the first and third needles, and the remaining half are on the second. The first st of the round should still begin the first needle. The second needle will be the back; the 2 short needles, the palm. K 1 round dk, increasing 1 (0, 1, 0) sts both front and back.

Start pattern and thumb gore in the next round: On the first needle, k 1 dk, k 1 lt, across. On the second needle work 3 (3½, 4, 4) blocks of pattern. On the sizes that don't quite fit, add enough sts *from the needle on the little-finger side* to finish the block of pattern.

For the right mitten, on the third needle k 1 lt, k 1 dk, k 1 lt, k 1 dk, k 1 lt, k 1 dk, then k 2 lt. The first lt st and last 2 lt sts mark the base of the thumb gore. K across in Salt and Pepper.

For the left mitten, k up to 8 sts before the end of round, then k 2 lt, k 1 dk, k 1 lt, k 1 dk, k 1 lt, k 1 dk, k 1 lt. The first 2 lt sts and the last lt st mark the base of the thumb gore.

K across palm in Salt and Pepper. If the pattern doesn't meet properly in the middle of the palm, inc 1 st, in this round only, by knitting both colors into 1 st.

Inc 1 st each side within the marking lines every second round 3 (3, 3, 4) times by knitting both colors into the lt st forming the inside of the marker, or if this won't work, into the st next to it.
Total after incs: 11 (11, 11, 14) thumb gore sts between the marking sts.

K up for a total of 10 (12, 14, 16) rounds, then put on a string all the sts within but not including the 2 lt lines. Cast on 5 sts over the gap and k straight up until mitten measures 2¾ (3, 3½, 4¼) inches above the cuff, or to the middle of the nail on the ring finger.

Dec: On both sides of palm and back (that is, not in the middle of the palm but at all other needle ends), k 2 together in pattern every other round once, then every round. When there are about 20 sts left, k 2 together around, following the pattern as closely as you can without starting a new band. Break yarn, and with a yarn needle draw the remaining sts up on the strand in the main color. Carry the other tail to the inside, then darn the mc back and forth invisibly over the tip.

Thumb: Pick up 11 (11, 11, 14) sts from string. Pick up and k 7 sts from back and corners of thumb hole. Inc 1 (1, 1, 0) sts to make an uneven number of sts, straight up in Salt and Pepper pattern for ¾ (1, 1¼, 1½) inches.

Dec sharply: K 2 together around until 6 to 8 sts remain. Break yarn and finish as on hand.

Draw all tails into the mitten, turn it inside out and darn them in securely. Trim off what's left.

Chipman's Block Tiny Mittens

Materials: About ¾ ounce dk and ½ ounce lt sportweight yarn (called fingering in Canada), preferably wool.

Equipment: 1 set U.S. no. 3 (Can. no. 10) dp knitting needles, or size needed to knit gauge. 1 set U.S. no. 1 (Can. no. 13) dp knitting needles for ribbed cuff. Yarn needle for finishing.

Gauge: 9 sts = 1 inch in Chipman's Block pattern.

Sizes: Instructions are for 6 months to 1 year. Instructions for sizes, 2, 3, and 4 years old are in parentheses.

Pattern: Chipman's Block, a multiple of 6 sts and 8 rounds, consists of 2 rounds of k 3 dk, k 3 lt followed by 2 rounds of Salt and Pepper (k 1 lt, k 1 dk, reversed in the second round), followed by 2 more rounds of k 3 lt, k 3 dk, followed by 2 more rounds of Salt and Pepper. The Salt and Pepper st above or below the center st of each 3-st block is the same color as the block, creating the impression of little diamonds. The overall impression is of a gingham check.

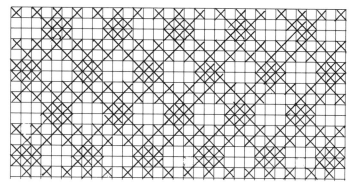

A very delicate pattern well-suited to baby mittens and caps.

Please read General Instructions for Double Knitting before starting this project.

Cuff: On smaller needles and using dk yarn, cast on 40 (48, 52, 56) sts. K 2, p 2 for 1¼ (1½, 1¾, 2) inches.

Change to larger needles. K 1 round in dk, increasing 2 (0, 2, 4) sts.

Start pattern: K to first round of Salt and Pepper, then inc for thumb.

Thumb gore: For the right mitten, the first 6 sts of the first needle are the beginning of the thumb gore. For the left mitten, it's the last 6 sts of the third needle. Above the 3 dk sts, inc twice in the first round of Salt and Pepper by knitting both colors, in the right order, into 2 adjacent sts. In the second round, k both colors into all 4 of these sts, making a total of 6 new sts in 2 rounds. For size 4, repeat this inc in the second band of Salt and Pepper.

K straight up in pattern until there are 8 (12, 12, 16) rounds, or 2 (3, 3, 4) 4-round bands of pattern.

Take off for thumb: On the second Salt and Pepper round, before knitting them, take off 11 (11, 11, 15) of the thumb gore sts and put them on a string or a safety pin.

Cast on 5 sts over the gap in pattern and k straight up in pattern until mitten measures 2¾ (3¼, 3¾, 4) inches from top of cuff.

Dec: In the middle of the *next* Salt and Pepper round, k 2 together 6 times on the little-finger side. K 1 more round Salt and Pepper and 1 more round k 3 lt, k 3 dk.

In the second round of k 3 lt, k 3 dk, k the first of each group of 3 sts normally, then k the second 2 sts together in the same color. Do this all the way around.

118

Next rounds, k Salt and Pepper: K 2 together around, twice, or until only about 10 to 14 sts remain. Break yarn with a 6-inch tail.

With a yarn needle, draw the remaining sts firmly up on the dk tail. Draw the lt tail into the mitten, then darn the dk tail back and forth across the tip, smoothly and invisibly.

Thumb: On 2 needles, pick up the 11 (11, 11, 15) sts from the thumb gore. With a third needle, pick up and k 7 sts from the back and corners of the thumb hole, being careful to match the pattern (Salt and Pepper). If the pattern doesn't quite work, as in the 4-year-old's size, either inc 2 immediately or hide the imperfection on the inside of the thumb. Continue Chipman's Block pattern straight up for ¾ (1, 1¼, 1½) inches, taking care not to pull yarn too tightly on the k 3 dk, k 3 lt rounds.

Dec sharply: If you now have a Salt and Pepper round coming up, k 1, k 2 together around in Salt and Pepper for 2 rounds. If you have the first 3 lt/3 dk round coming up, k it without decreasing, then in the second round k 1 dk, k 2 together in dk, k 1 lt, k 2 together in lt, around. Then k 2 together around in Salt and Pepper until 6 to 8 sts remain. Finish off as you did on the hand.

Finishing: Draw all tails into the mitten, darn them securely and neatly into the inside surface, and trim the ends off. Turn it right side out and it's ready to wear.

Partridge Chicky Feet Mittens

This is the most charming pattern I've seen, call it "crow's feet" or "hen tracks" or "partridge." It comes from Down East, around Blue Hill and Searsport, Maine, where I've heard it's often sold at church fairs.

It promotes the farming and hunting tradition of Maine and binds us back to our state's soil.

As a baby pattern, it's perfect. I'd like to use it someday as a sweater design with little chicks or partridges across the shoulders.

Remember to catch up the light strand on the long leaps in the middle of each set of feet, or little fingers will get caught!

—R.H.

Partridge Chicky Feet Mittens

About ¾ ounce dk and ½ ounce lt sportweight (Canadian fingering weight) yarn, preferably wool.

Equipment: 1 set U.S. no. 2 (Can. no. 11) dp knitting needles, or size you need to k the pattern to gauge. 1 set U.S. no. 1 (Can. no. 13) dp knitting needles for ribbed cuff. Yarn needle for finishing.

Gauge: 9 sts = 1 inch in Partridge pattern.

Sizes: Instructions are for size one year. Instructions for sizes 2 and 4 are in parentheses. Sizes 6 months to one year and 3 years don't work with this pattern without some trickiness, but if you're willing to fiddle with this, subtract half a pattern element (4 sts) from the next larger size and decrease the length of hand and thumb and

thumb gore halfway to the next smaller size.

Pattern: Partridge is a multiple of 8 sts and 8 rounds. It can be k flat, with an extra st added to each edge for the seam.

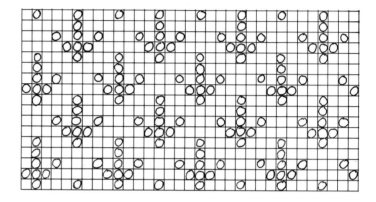

Please read General Instructions for Double-Knitting before starting this project.

Cuff: Using dk yarn and Maine method, cast on 40 (48, 56) sts onto smaller needles. K 2, p 2 (or k 3, p 1) for 1½ (1¾, 2¼) inches.

Change to larger needles and start pattern. K 2 rounds of pattern and begin inc for thumb gore.

Thumb gore: The first 8 sts of the first needle for the right mitten, and the last 8 sts of the third needle for the left mitten, form the base of the thumb gore. Put a marker between the eighth and the ninth sts if you have trouble keeping track. Follow the thumb gore graph, knitting right across the large gaps in the graph as if they didn't exist. In fact, they don't, but are only there to show you where to inc. Inc by knitting both colors into the same st on both sides of the center st if this works in the pattern, or if there's no handy color change in which to work this kind of inc, k into the st

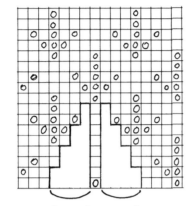

Thumb increase detail.

directly under the next st, then the usual next st, on both sides of the center st.

When you have increased 4 times (8 new sts) and have 16 sts between your thumb gore marker and the end of the needle, k straight up 2 more rounds. Put 15 of the thumb gore sts on a string or a safety pin. Cast on 7 sts over the gap and k straight up in pattern until 2¾ (3¼, 3¾) inches above the cuff.

Dec: Start with the first round of a row of feet. You will have both the heels of the new feet and the toes of the old, thus it will be k 3 dk, k 1 lt (or k 1 lt, k 3 dk, depending on which set of feet you're on). K a toe st then *k 1 dk, k 2 together dk, k 1 lt (a heel). K 1 dk, k 2 together dk, k 1 lt (a toe)*. Repeat this around.

Second dec round: K 2 of the dk sts together between all the new feet and k the 3 lt sts for the new feet as charted.

Third dec round: The round on your needles will be 3 lt, 2 dk. Instead of making the lt triangles into feet, make them into little diamonds: in the center of each group of 3 lt sts, k 1 lt and k the next 2 sts together dk, and the *next* 2 sts again together dk. Repeat this around and you will have 1 lt, 2 dk around when you're finished.

Break the lt yarn, stuff it inside the mitten, and k 1, k 2 together dk around until 10 to 12 sts remain. Break dk yarn, draw the remaining sts up on the tail, and darn it back and forth over the tip in the dk sts, taking care to keep your sts smooth and invisible. Darn all ends into the back of the fabric.

Thumb: On three needles, pick up the 15 thumb gore sts from the string and 11 (yes, 11) from the back and corners. Make the pattern work in front and on the inside of the thumb, but make the 2 sts on each corner the same color and k them together in the next round. Total: 24 sts. This is rather a large thumb for the smallest size, so in that size knit it on needles 1 size smaller to make it narrower. You can do this for the middle size too, if the thumb seems too wide.

K straight up for ¾ (1, 1¼) inches. Dec either as on the hand or knit 1, k 2 together around twice, matching colors as best you can. Finish as on the hand.

Petites Mitaines en Fleur-de-lis

These little mittens are simply smaller versions of the adult Fleur-de-lis mittens. They're a good first project in double knitting: they have no thumb gore, but make up for this in extra width to allow for the thumb. They also have only one color on the thumb and one color at the tip of the mitten, after the double-knit pattern has stopped. They take very little time to knit, and you'll have time to make a matching cap.

Petites Mitaines en Fleur-de-lis

Materials: The example in the color photo is knit in a mixture of yarns. The navy blue and white yarns are Brunswick Pomfret Sport Yarn; the gray, a fingering weight yarn from Bartlettyarns, and the pale blue is a single-ply medium fingering from Canada via the American company Candide. Slight differences in loft and thickness don't seem to matter much in this tiny pattern. You will need ½ to ¾ ounce light sportweight (fingering) yarn, preferably wool, and small amounts of three contrasting colors. I used two rather bland colors and one bright contrast to make one band of lilies stand out clearly in each series, as this was the effect of the adult mitten I have in four colors.

Equipment: 1 set U.S. no. 1 (Can. no. 13) dp knitting needles for the ribbed cuff. 1 set U.S. no. 3 (Can. no. 10) dp knitting needles, or *size needed to knit the correct gauge.*

Gauge: 9 sts = 1 inch in Fleur-de-lis pattern.

Sizes: Directions are for size newborn to 6 months. Directions for sizes 6 months to 1 year, 2, 3, and 4 are in parentheses.

Pattern: In 2 colors, Fleur-de-lis is a 4-st by 6-round pattern. In 4 colors, it repeats every 18 rounds. It can be k flat if desired, but be sure to allow an extra st on each side for the seam. The only incs come before the beginning of the pattern; and decs are in empty spaces between motifs at the tip. Carry the contrast colors ahead.

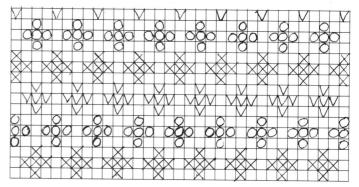

For additional hints, see the directions for the adult Fleur-de-lis Mitten.

Please read General Instructions for Double Knitting before starting this project.

Cuff: On 3 of the smaller needles, cast on 40 (44, 48, 52, 56) sts in lt yarn. K 2, p 2 for 1¼ (1½, 1¾, 2, 2¼) inches.

Change to larger needles and k one round lt, increasing 4 sts, spaced evenly.

Begin pattern. K 3 bands of lilies before thumb hole, twisting the contrast colors together behind your work with a single twist at the end of each band.

Consider making thumbless mittens if the baby is under nine months. To do this, simply omit the next step. There will be plenty of room for a little fist in these.

Thumb hole: At the beginning of the round for the right mitten and the end of the round for the left mitten, k a short piece of completely different yarn onto (7, 8, 9, 10) sts, tucking tails from both ends inside the mitten. Backtrack and reknit these sts in pattern. (Later you will pick out the short piece of yarn and have an equal number of sts on top and bottom of a thumb hole.)

K straight up in pattern until mitten measures 2¼ (2¾, 3¼, 3¾, 4¼) inches above cuff. K up to the third pattern round, then dec: K 1 lt, k 2 dk sts together, k 2 lt. Repeat this around.

Next round, break dk yarns and k 1 lt, k 2 together lt around and around until about 8 sts remain.

Break yarn with a 6-inch tail, thread the tail onto a yarn needle, and draw the remaining sts up firmly. Darn back and forth over the tip, following the shapes of the knitted sts to make the darn invisible.

Thumb: Pick out the extra length of yarn carefully. On 3 of the larger needles and with lt yarn, pick up (7, 8, 9, 10) sts from the front of thumb hole, pick up and k the same number from the back, and pick up and k 1 st from each corner by twisting a side loop of a st there. Total: (16, 18, 20, 22) sts.

K straight up in lt yarn for (¾, 1, 1¼, 1½) inches. Dec sharply: K 1, k 2 together for 2 or 3 rounds, until only 8 to 12 sts remain. Draw these up on a yarn needle and finish as you did on the hand.

Draw all ends to the inside of the mitaine, turn it inside out and darn all ends into the inside surface of the fabric. If you have a little hole on each corner of the thumb hole, use 2 of these tails to darn it neatly and inconspicuously. A darning egg or a small round stone will be helpful as a backing to your darning. Use a narrow broom handle or other such to darn against on the thumb.

Very nice! Now knit another!

Patterned Cap

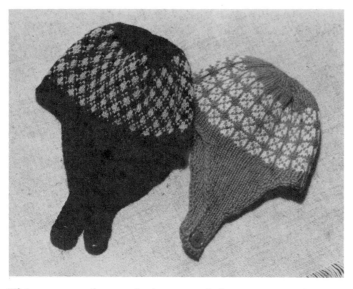

This cap can be made in any of the patterns given here for babies and little children. It is the same set of instructions given in *Fox & Geese & Fences* (Down East Books, 1983) and is taken from a little Danish cap belonging to my children. The examples are in Chipman's Block and Fox and Geese.

—R.H.

Patterned Cap

Materials: About 1½ ounce dk and ¾ ounce lt sportweight yarn (called fingering in Canada). One ⅜-inch button.

Equipment: 1 set U.S. no. 2 (Can. no. 11) dp or straight knitting needles for ribbing. For the rest of the cap, 1 set no. 4 (Can. no. 9) dp or straight knitting needles, or size needed to knit correct gauge. All the patterns *except* Compass can be knit flat if you wish.

Gauge: 8½ inches = 1 inch in pattern.

Sizes: Newborn to 6 months (6 months to 1½ year, 2 to 4 years old). This corresponds to a finished hat circumference of 14 (16, 18) inches.

See the mitten instructions for the pattern you wish to use and read the accompanying pattern notes.

Be sure to read General Instructions for Double Knitting, if you haven't already, before starting.

This cap is knit from the top down.

Cast on 15 (17, 20) sts in dk yarn, divided among 3 of the smaller knitting needles. In the next round, inc 1 in every st. Total 30 (34, 40) sts.

Then rib: K 1, p 1 around. Rib 3 rounds.

In the next round, inc in every st. Total 60 (68, 80) sts.

Then rib 5 rounds, k 1, p 1.

In the next round, inc in every st until there are 120 (136, 156) sts. For any pattern based on a multiple of 6 sts, add 2 more sts in the next round for the second size only. For multiples of 7 sts, inc 1 st less (3 less, 2 less). For multiples of 10, inc to the nearest multiple of 10, either larger or smaller. (You may be adding almost ½ inch, so be careful. Measure the child's head if possible. The cap can be up to 1 inch smaller but not much bigger than the child's head.)

Rib 2 more rounds, k 1, p 1, then change to larger needles.

K 1 round dk.

Start pattern: K in pattern of your choice for 2⅝ (3, 3½) inches, or as near as possible. Do complete the pattern. Finish with 1 round of dk.

Change to smaller needles and k 1, p 1 for 6 rounds.

Bind off: Bind off 17 (19, 22) sts at the beginning of round for back of cap. K 1, p 1 across 34 (39, 45) sts for ear tab. Bind off 35 (39, 44) sts for front of cap. K 1, p 1 across 34 (39, 45) sts for second ear tab. For multiples of 6, 7, or 10, add or subtract from the ear tabs the sts that adjusted for the pattern—half the number on each one.

On 1 ear tab, continue k 1, p 1 ribbing back and forth, decreasing 1 st at end of every row until the tab is 2 (2¼, 2½) inches below the edge of the brim. Then dec 1 st at both ends of every row until 8 (10, 10) sts remain. Continue to rib back and forth for 1½ (1¾, 2) more inches. Bind off.

Repeat on the other ear tab.

For boy's cap, using tail from knitting, crochet a buttonloop on the end of the left ear tab. For a girl's cap, crochet a buttonloop on the end of the right ear tab, using the tail from knitting. For both, continue to single crochet all the way around the edge of the cap until you reach the buttonloop again. Single crochet around this too, making it stronger, then tie off just beyond it.

Work all loose ends into the back of the fabric. Using the tail from casting on and a yarn needle, catch up all the cast-on sts at the top of the crown and draw them up firmly, so there's no hole. Darn invisibly and smoothly back and forth over the top.

Acknowledgments

Any collection of traditional processes must be the work of more than one person. It takes generations of craftspersons to carry a tradition into the present, people like myself and the publishers to see the need to present the process to the wider public in a book, and it takes a state, or a region, of people hungry for roots to sink deeper into a native soil. Most of all, it takes the willingness of living craftspeople to share what amounts to privileged family craft techniques and lore with thousands of people they will never see or know.

To thank the knitters of the past and present for maintaining traditional knitting designs is superfluous, as their reward is in the pleasure of knitting and the love of those who wear their creations. Janetta and I thank those in the present generation who shared family knitting traditions: Edna Mower, of Merrimack, New Hampshire, and Beulah Moore, of Kingfield, Maine, for Double-rolled Mittens; Mrs. Nathan Richardson, of Hudson, Massachusetts, for information about Shagged Loggers' Mittens; Albert Miller, of Turner, Maine, for Mittens Hooked on a Dowel; Erin Pender for helping to figure out Mittens with Shag on the Inside; Barbara H.P. Wells, of Coraopolis, Pennsylvania, for the All-Cuff Wristers; Pat Flaherty, of Blue Hill, Maine, for Partridge Feet Mittens; Bertha York, of Harpswell, Maine, for local information on Compass Mittens; Margaret Richard and Annie Pettipas, of Charlos Cove, Nova Scotia, for Fleur-de-lis Mittens; Harriet Pardy Martin, of Happy Valley, Labrador, for the basic instructions for the Newfoundland-Labrador Mittens, and Phyllis Montague, of Northwest River, Labrador, for sharing her mother's patterns, Shining Star and Big Waves. Thanks also to the woman in Brunswick, Maine, who showed me a pair of tiny silk mittens with Peek-a-boo and striped patterns. I met her only briefly and didn't get her name, but I have copied her mittens, which are presented here as Cunnin' Old-timey Baby Mittens.

In addition, we thank the many women in Atlantic Canada who shared with Janetta patterns that she has passed on in this book, particularly Mrs. Viette Cruikshank, of Liscomb, Nova Scotia, for the Mattie Owl story and pattern (which is also Compass), and Mrs. Murdock Hollingsworth, of Truro, Nova Scotia, for information about Flying Geese gloves.

We also thank the Nova Scotia Museum for letting us use patterns that appeared in Janetta's book **Traditional Nova Scotian Double-Knitting Patterns** (Halifax, 1985): Flying Geese, Diamond and Fleur-de-lis, and Maplewood; *Them Days* magazine for permission to reprint the interview and photo of Harriet Pardy Martin; the Maine State Museum for permission to print their photos and information on Double-rolled Mittens, Shagged Logger's Mitts, and shagged sleigh driver's mittens. Joan Waldron, of the Nova Scotia Museum, who has become a good friend, put me in touch with knitting traditions in Nova Scotia and introduced me to Janetta Dexter; Jane Nylander, textile curator of Old Sturbridge Village, and Jane Radcliffe, textile curator of the Maine State Museum, both helped by giving me access to their collections and expanding my general knowledge of traditional mitten knitting in their areas.

Thanks to Elizabeth Zimmermann and her daughter, Meg Swanson, the *doyennes* of American knitting design, for advice on publication, for contacts, for providing many books on British, Scandinavian, and German knitting, and most of all, for saying nice things about my books in the knitting world.

Thanks to Professor Anthony Barrand of the University Professors Program at Boston University for caring about my slightly bizarre field of study, for teaching me better ways of documenting interviews and new (to me) methods of observation, and for general encouragement. Thanks to the University Professors Program for taking me in and allowing me to deepen my study of traditional handcraft processes.

I would also like to thank Nora Johnson, of Five Islands, Maine, who was the first traditional knitter willing to talk to me about Maine double-knit patterns, and who taught me my first three patterns. She has commented on and reviewed all the mittens I have found in various corners of New England and Canada, and as a seasoned knitter has checked some of the patterns for me for readability. Her insistence on high-quality workmanship and technique in mitten knitting continues to guide my eyes and hands.

Like other authors, I have a family, who have not only put up with all my nonsense, but have also helped produce this book: my husband, Erik, helped with the more mathematical aspects of figuring sizes, my daughter Janine produced some of the instructional diagrams from photographs, my son Morten and my daughter Hanne pushed shutters and wore mittens for the black-and-white photographs. All of them, and my son Bear, wore mittens for the color photographs.

Especially many thanks to my co-author, Janetta Dexter, of Annapolis County, Nova Scotia. Janetta became the Canadian clearing house for double-knit patterns after her self-published, mimeographed **Traditional Nova Scotian Double-Knitting Patterns** sold out a printing of 1000 in a single summer, without benefit of modern marketing techniques.

Although she has knit mittens and gloves most of her life and furnishes her home mostly by a variety of handiwork, Janetta considers herself more a genealogist and spinner-dyer than a knitter. It was as a former teacher and local history buff that she produced **Double-Knitting Patterns,** hoping simply to record a few of the patterns she had learned growing up in Lunenburg County and from other knitters she met at sheep shows in Nova Scotia. Neither she nor her neighbor Betty Hearn, who worked with her on the first edition, had any idea that it would be received and used as a pattern book by thousands of knitters in the United States and Canada, or that it would draw the attention of knitting history enthusiasts as far away as England. Reprinted repeatedly by the Nova Museum, it was recently republished by them as a small printed book, with black-and-white photographs.

I have always felt welcome in Janetta's and Willy's home, and her kindness in preparing patterns for this book, in knitting mittens, and helping to edit portions of the book has been unbounded. Many, many thanks!

Also, thanks to you, dear knitters, for making these mittens and becoming the tradition-bearers of them for new generations. The best reward for writing these books has been later to see "my" mittens on children playing in the snow in New Hampshire, or on a woman shopping in Portland, or on the hands of a student waiting for a trolley in Boston.

—Robin Hansen

Bibliography

Sources on North American Folk Knitting

Marlene Davis, et al. **A Nova Scotia Workbasket: Some Needlework Patterns Traditionally Used in the Province.** Halifax, Nova Scotia: Nova Scotia Museum, 1976. 113 pp., illustrated with b/w photos and diagrams. Bibliography, sources of supply, and accession numbers referring to museum artifacts shown.

Workbasket includes knitting, weaving, rugmaking, quilting, crochet, and embroidery. The knitting section comprises socks, mittens (fishermen's and two-ball instructions provided), a hug-me-tight, or sleeved shawl, nippers, knitted blankets and afghans, and knitted rugs.

Janetta Dexter. **Traditional Nova Scotian Double-Knitting Patterns.** Halifax: Nova Scotia Museum, 1972, 1985. Illus. with graphs, black-and-white photos of fabric.

Robin Hansen. **Fox & Geese & Fences: A Collection of Traditional Maine Mittens.** Camden, Me.: Down East Books, 1982. 72 pp., illustrated with b/w and color photos and graphs. No bibliography.

Doris Saunders. "Labrador Crafts: Finger Mitts," in **Them Days: Stories of Early Labrador,** VI, no. 3, 1981, pp. 50–51. Illustrated with b/w photos and small graphs.

An oral account by Harriet Pardy Martin, of Happy Valley, Labrador, telling how to make a traditional Labrador finger mitt, or shooting glove, with a traditional Labrador diamond design in two-colored knitting.

Gerald L. Pocius. **Textile Traditions of Eastern Newfoundland.** Canadian Centre for Folk Culture Studies Paper no. 29. Ottawa: National Museums of Canada, 1979. 112 pp., illustrated with b/w photos. Bibliography.

Pocius' study of the folk textile traditions in Eastern Newfoundland relies heavily on oral accounts, and brings much new information to public attention. A folklorist, he presents knitting, weaving, and crochet traditions, but he is a little short on technology. The book cannot really be used as a how-to or pattern book, but is good reading.

Sources on British and Irish Folk Knitting

Michael Harvey and Rae Compton. **Fisherman Knitting, Shire Album 31: Full Instructions for Knitting Four Garments.** Aylesbury: Shire Publications Ltd., 1978. 33 pp., illustrated with b/w photos and graphs. Short bibliography.

History of folklore surrounding the "gansey," also the British method of knitting with a knitting sheath. Instructions are given for two ganseys, one Aran, and one Fair Isle pullover.

Sheila McGregor. **Traditional Knitting.** London: Batsford Ltd., 1983. Illustrated with color photos. 66 pp.

Here now a surprise—an authoritative history of knitting with no instructions for anything. Modern knitting follows Scandinavian and British traditions.

————. **The Complete Book of Traditional Fair Isle Knitting.** New York: Charles Scribner's Sons, 1982. 141 pp. illustrated with color and b/w photos, many graphs and diagrams. Bibliography, index.

This excellent book concentrates solely on the banded bicolor patterns of Fair Isle, with tons of background, graphs of patterns, and everything you would ever want to know on the subject.

Gwyn Morgan. **Traditional Knitting: Patterns of Ireland, Scotland, and England.** New York: St. Martin's Press, 1981. Also London: Ward Lock Ltd., 1981. 119 pp., illustrated with color and b/w photos.

Although there are ten pages of background, including a wrongish history of knitting, this is mainly an instruction book. The knitting here is not the traditional in-the-round method, but the printed instruction method of make-a-back-make-a-front-make-two-sleeves-and-sew-everything-together. There are 31 patterns, including one for fingerless gloves, the only handwear in the book.

Michael Pearson. **Michael Pearson's Traditional Knitting: Aran, Fair Isle and Fisher Ganseys.** New York: Van Nostrand Reinhold Company, 1984. Also London: William Collins Sons & Company Ltd., 1984. 204 pp., richly illustrated with b/w and color photos, graphs and line drawings (to show details of the mainly navy blue sweaters). Bibliography.

Pearson has collected all the information in his earlier little works on fishermen's sweaters on the east coast of the British Isles and added more, plus much improved photo production. Like his earlier books, follows the coastline geographically, giving facts of coastal interest and economy as well as what the fishermen wear.

If Pearson seems a little thin on technique—he doesn't seem to notice who does what and how—he still has a marvelous presentation of the history of English and Scottish (and Shetland, Orkney, and Faeroe) knitting, and lots of quotations from old sources.

Gladys Thompson. **Patterns for Guernseys, Jerseys, and Arans: Fishermen's Sweaters from the British Isles.** New York: Dover Publications (reprint), 1969, 1979. London: B. T. Batsford Ltd., 1969. The original did not include Aran at all, not even in the title. 173 pp., illustrated with b/w photos and graphs.

This is the original and classic collection of fishermen's patterns from the British Isles. Thompson traveled to the islands and harbors there collecting instructions, lore, designs, and photographs for this book. Her account includes much delightful chatter about her travels, as well as oral commentary from the knitters and wearers of the sweaters. She was my role model.

There are instructions for all the many sweaters shown.

Mary Wright. **Cornish Guernseys and Knit-frocks.** Penzance: Alison Hodge in association with Ethnographica Ltd., 1979. (Not examined.)

Sources on Scandinavian Folk Knitting

"Course: Norwegian Knitting: Gloves and Mitts in Norwegian Patterns," **Anna: Burda Knitting and Needlecrafts,** November 1982.

A useful six-page pullout on correct techniques of Norwegian two-colored knitting, with several very different varieties of Scandinavian hand-wear and several matching two-colored hats. Excellently illustrated technical information of every sort, and authentic patterns.

Included are traditional popular Norwegian mittens with large motifs on the back of the hand, all-over checked mittens, and mittens and gloves with bands of pattern either only at the cuff or all over the mitten.

Annichen Sibbern Bohn. **Norwegian Knitting Designs.** Oslo: Grondahl & Son, Publishers, 1952. 64 pp., illustrated with b/w photographs, graphs.

A collection of traditional Norwegian graphed knitting patterns, with only the motifs graphed—that is, there is no graph for an entire mitten or sock showing the increases, decreases, etc., nor are there written instructions to follow. This is available in reprint.

Pauline Chatterton. **Scandinavian Knitting Designs.** New York: Charles Scribner's Sons, 1977. 264 pp., illustrated with b/w photos, graphs, instructive diagrams, 8 pp. color photos. Index.

Most of the 124 pages of designs have no commentary, no indication of whether they came from the northern British Isles, Norway, Iceland, Sweden, or Denmark. She gives no names to the patterns, which often have descriptive names in the families that knit them.

For the knitter, there are a lot of fun patterns, without, however, the fun of knowing their background, and there are instructions for knitting various garments and household items, but not traditional in-the-round garments.

Dale Yarn Company. **Knit Your Own Norwegian Sweaters: Complete Instructions for 50 Authentic Sweaters, Hats, Mittens, Gloves, Caps, Etc.** New York: Dover Publications, 1974. (Also printed in Canada. Toronto: General Publishing Company Ltd. Originally published in Norway as **Knit It Yourself.** Oslo: J. W. Cappelens Forlag, 1966.) 58 pp., illustrated with instructive drawings, b/w and color photos and graphs.

An oldy but goody, Knit Your Own passes on real traditional Norwegian knitting techniques and gives instructions for finishing circular knits by stitching and slitting the knit fabric, also for stranding—knitting two colors with two hands without getting tangled up.

Some of the sweaters are a little dated; others aren't and will last forever.

Eva Maria Leszner. **Vantar Fran Nar och Fjarran** (Mittens from Near and Far). Swedish, but translated from German and adapted by Eva Trotzig. Stockholm: LTs Forlag, 1981. 93 pp., illustrated with color and b/w photos and graphs. Originally published as **Handschuhe, Mutzen, und Schals farbig gestrickt** (Gloves, Mittens, and Mufflers Knitted in Color). Rosenheim: Rosenheimer Verlagshaus Alfred Forg GmbH & Co KG, 1980.

Leszner's book stands alone as the best international collection of mittens in a single publication, and many of the graphed patterns can be used for actual knitting.

Lizbeth Upitis. **Latvian Mittens: Traditional Designs and Techniques. Latviesu Cimdi: Raksti un Technikas.** Bilingual publication. St. Paul, Minn.: Dos Tejedoras, 1981. 78 pp., illustrated with four-page color spread, many charted two- and three-color designs. Bibliography, index.

Contains fifteen pages on the cultural importance of mittens in Latvia, and other background material. Well researched, beautifully written and illustrated, with abundant regional and village citations.

The Swedish Mitten Book: Traditional Patterns from Gotland. Asheville, N.C.: Lark Books, 1984. First published in Sweden under the title **Gotlandska Stickmonster** (Gotlandic Knitting Patterns) by Almqvist & Wiksell Forlag A/B, 1981. 103 pp., illustrated with b/w photos and graphs.

This book was not originally intended as a mitten book, but mittens were used as a convenient means of conveying the small geometric patterns.

This book revolutionized my research, as it contained no fewer than five patterns identical to Canadian and Maine small geometric patterns. I had previously found only spotty indications of a Swedish communality with the Canadian and Maine patterns. I then began to look more closely at the idea of a British origin for them and was led to many new sources.

This is an unassuming little collection of patterns, neatly traced by specific location within Gotland, nicely illustrated with mittens rather than swatches. Basic instructions are included for mittens using several sizes of yarn and knitting tensions.

Britta Johansson and Kersti Nilsson. **Binge—en Hallansk Sticktradition.** (Binge—a Halland Knitting Tradition) In Swedish. Stockholm: LTs Forlag, 1980. 118 pp., illustrated with color and b/w photos, graphs and a few instructive line drawings.

A wealth of historical information and photographs and exquisitely detailed directions, including blocking, shrinking, and washing instructions.

Binge *means simply "knitting" in the Hallandsk dialect, from the Scandinavian word "binde," which initially meant* nalbindning, *but came to be applied to knitting as well in many outlying areas when knitting replaced* nalbindning.

Binge *has a nice history of Halland knitting tradition, including much museum work and examination of old documents. Also includes many historical photos of people knitting.*

Vibeke Lind. **Knit in the Nordic Tradition.** Asheville, N.C.: Lark Books, 1984. (Originally published in Danish: **Strik med Nordisk Tradition.** Copenhagen: Host & Soen, 1981, 1982.) 127 pp., illustrated with color and b/w photos, graphs, and many instructive diagrams and sketches.

Very slick, very good, this book contains everything basic one ever wanted to know about the better-known aspects of Scandinavian folk knitting. Lots of historical photos and museum artifacts, lots of instructions for everything from spiral-ribbed stockings to Norwegian lusekofte *pullovers. The instructions are very terse, however, and may be inaccessible to those of us who are accustomed to being told everything.*

A large section in the beginning gives traditional technical instructions (how to knit in the round, how to knit in two colors, how to knit with two strands, how to felt knitted fabric). A photo of handsome Arctic explorer Knud Rasmussen wearing a double-knit sweater is worth the price of the book.

Marika Larsson. **Stickat fran Norrbotten: Vantar, Sockor, och Mossor.** (Knitted in Norbotten: Mittens, Socks, and Caps.) In Swedish. Stockholm: LTs Forlag, 1978. 60 pp., illustrated with b/w and color photos and graphs.

Good background material, oral interviews, with people in the Swedish province closest to the Finnish border. The illustrations show individual imagination and various ethnic influences at play—Swedish, Norwegian, Lappish (colors!), and Finnish.

There are two basic instructions for mittens to which a wealth of two- and three-color patterns can be added, and patterns for the several caps and ankle-high socks.

Kajsa Lindquist. **Scandinavian Snow Sets: Caps, Mittens, Gloves, After-Ski Boots and Slipper Socks,** vol. 5. 37 pp., illustrated with b/w photos and graphs. Exclusive distributor, Nomis Yarn Company, 53 Tosca Drive, Stoughton, MA, 02072. Published by Plays, Inc., Publishers, 1947, but still being reprinted and widely used.

For years this was the only source available in the United States of instructions for two-colored Scandinavian mittens and hats. This is exclusively an instruction book with a brief introduction.

Excellent instructions, easy to use, but each design is available in only one or two sizes.

Kajsa Lindquist and Natalie Hebert. **Nomis Scandinavian Sweaters.** 1946. 30 pp., illustrated with b/w photographs and graphs.

Again, this was for years the only American source for Scandinavian two-colored sweater instructions. Still reprinted and widely used.

Sheila McGregor. **The Complete Book of Traditional Scandinavian Knitting.** Foreword by the Bishop of Leicester. New York: St. Martin's Press, 1984. Also London: B. T. Batsford Ltd., 1984. 168 pp., richly illustrated with many b/w and some color photos, diagrams, graphs. Index, glossary, bibliography.

An excellent detailed account of all the generally known printed sources on Scandinavian knitting, including Norway, Sweden, Denmark, and the North Atlantic islands—Faeroe and Iceland. McGregor includes plenty of patterns for knitters to play with, a glossary of English and Scandinavian knitting terms, and a bibliography that includes almost everything in this bibliography!

Ann Moeller Nielsen. **Pregle, Binde, og Laenke— Gammel Dansk Strikketradition.** (Old Danish Knitting Traditions.) In Danish. Fredericia, Denmark: Ann Moeller Nielsen, 1983. 119 pp., illustrated with b/w photos, drawings, and graphs. Bibliography.

Much original research and some museum research on the use of knitting in Danish folk costume in earlier times including direct quotations of old poems, songs, bits and snatches of diaries, and old-time knitting instructions. Also the history of knitting as a cottage industry in Denmark, and old knitting tools no longer in use.

This book is valuable for its original research and its use of different material (from all the rest). It has a very complete bibliography as well. Lots of old photos and reproductions of paintings showing knit garments in native Danish clothing.

Anna Petersson-Berg. **Monsterstickning (Bindslojd): Fullstandig Larokurs Jamte Monster.** (Patterned

Knitting: A Complete Course with Patterns.) In Swedish. Stockholm: Ahlen & Akerlunds Forlag, 1924. 87 pp., illustrated with b/w photos and graphs.

Regional folk patterns in two or more colors, identified by province. One of the earlier Swedish collections of bicolored patterns, specifically good because of the variety and the pinpointing of patterns by region. (Found at the Library of Congress.)

Gia Wiman-Ringquist, ed. **100 Landskapsvantar: ICA Kuriren.** (100 Mittens and Gloves from the Countryside: The ICA Contest.) In Swedish. Vasteras, Sweden: ICA Forlaget, 1982. 51 pp. Color photographs and graphs.

The results of a contest by ICA, a montly magazine, this softcover saddle-stitched book can excite even men about mittens! The colors are the bright complements and harmonies of Scandinavia, and the often unusual techniques are traditional to the provinces they represent. Included are bicolored patterns, mittens in nalbindning, potad *mittens (slip-stitch crocheted only through the front of each stitch), mittens lined with shagged loops, mittens with traveling stitches, crocheted, felt, and embroidered mittens, and two-strand (monotone) knitting.*

Sources of all mittens are cited by name and instructions are given for the 20 top winners, including all unusual techniques except two-strand knitting, nalbindning, *and felting. An address is supplied for information on two-strand knitting.*